THE ARABS

THE
ARABS

A LIVING HISTORY

BASIM MUSALLAM

COLLINS / HARVILL

8 GRAFTON STREET, LONDON W1

1983

Harvill Press Ltd
is distributed by
William Collins Sons & Co. Ltd
London · Glasgow · Sydney · Auckland
Toronto · Johannesburg

BRITISH LIBRARY CATALOGUING IN PUBLICATION DATA
Musallam, Basim
    The Arabs.
    1. Arabs – History
    I. Title
    909'. 04927   DS37.7

    ISBN 0-00-272010-8

CONTENTS

PREFACE

Why do people today from Morocco to Iraq call themselves Arabs? They do not live in one nation-state like the French in France or the Greeks in Greece. They do not all share the Muslim faith, and the majority of Muslims in the world are not Arabs. They are not a distinct race; culturally and geographically they adjoin peoples (Turks and Iranians for example) who have shared much of their history. Thus it is not because Arabs have no alternative, often powerful, definitions of identity current among them that they call themselves Arabs. There are black Arabs and white Arabs, Muslims, Christians, Africans, Asians, Sunnis, Shi'ites, overall a rich variety of geographical, religious, racial, social, political differences.

In the nineteenth century a native of Damascus or Jerusalem might have called himself an Ottoman, a Muslim, a Christian, but it is less likely that he would have called himself an 'Arab'. Modern Arab identity developed in the twentieth century as the result of an option taken, a course pursued. And it triumphed among the people who today call themselves Arabs.

Fourteen centuries ago the answer to the question of who are the Arabs would have been simple: they were the people who spoke Arabic and lived in the Arabian peninsula. Eleven centuries ago it was equally clear: inspired by the teachings of Mohammed, they had become the rulers of a vast empire stretching from Spain to Persia. In time most of those they ruled became Muslim and adopted the Arabic language, and more gradually an 'Arab' civilisation emerged, expressed in Arabic and through Islam, but also heir to the ancient traditions of the Near East, of Egypt and Babylon, Greece and Persia.

It was not very long before the Arabic-Islamic empire fell to pieces, giving way to a proliferation of independent rulers and autonomous or semi-autonomous governors. But when, in the early years of the twentieth century, Arab nationalist movements seethed under Ottoman rule, their standard was the heritage of the Arabic language and culture. Through a policy of Turkification, the Turks had tried to tighten their hold on what remained of the Ottoman empire. Instead they provoked a surge of Arab revivalism.

Between the birth of the idea of Arab independence in Syria and the destruction of that independence there are but a few years. The destruction of the nascent Syrian Arab state by the force of European arms after World War I involved the division of the land, and its people, according to the designs of Sykes-Picot and Balfour. Other Arab peoples, like those of Algeria, had long before experienced European domination and thus to the shared memory of a gloriously united Arab civilisation has been added another shared memory – a bitter one – that of European colonial rule.

This book, like the film series which it accompanies, attempts to show the Arab past as it still informs the minds and imaginations of Arabs today. The tensions between a proud distant past and a recent past that verges on the ignoble are strung throughout contemporary political and social discourse and inspire the questions that Arabs continually ask of themselves. Many of these questions are common to all 'Third World' societies – What is our relation to the West? How much can a society borrow from another without becoming another? But for the Arabs who were once the great resource of *other* nations, these questions have a special colouring.

What is equally significant is the range of spheres in which these questions arise. It is not only political leaders who pose them when they espouse open- and closed-door policies; they also seek to be resolved in the voices of women confronting the powerful influence of Western feminism; in the voices of urban planners considering the introduction of boulevards in Cairo; in the voices of poets trying to restore their language to its function as an authentic and expressive idiom of the people. And as the same questions are posed by a poet in Beirut and a novelist in Morocco, or a woman in Jordan and another in Kuwait, the historical dilemma of being Arab in this stage of the twentieth century becomes an important part of a collective identity. This book does not pretend to exhaust the levels of this dialogue within the Arab world, but it does hope to lead the reader to the point where he can listen from the inside.

* * *

What non-Arabs would like to know about the Arabs and what Arabs would want to say are not always the same. This book attempts to combine these two, often different perspectives. John Keay, a notable author in his own right, worked assiduously and with unfailing insight on the presentation of material which was itself the work of Arab writers and teachers, journalists and scholars, who have written and presented the documentary series. Without his collaboration during the busy months of filming any exposition of 'The Arabs' in book form would have been impossible. Indeed, his name properly belongs with mine on the cover of this book.

The authors of the film commentaries deserve particular mention and thanks with respect to the chapters they have influenced. For chapter 2, Khalida Said, literary critic and professor at the Lebanese University of Beirut; for chapter 3, Ali el Mek, writer and Director of the University of Khartoum Press; for chapter 4, Abdallah Hammoudi, social anthropologist and professor attached to the University of Rabat, Morocco; for chapter 5,

Galal Amin, teacher of economics at the American University in Cairo; for chapter 6, Abdulhamid Sabra, professor in the Department of History of Science at Harvard University; for chapter 7, Nadia Hijab, Editor-in-Chief of the monthly *The Middle East*, published in London; for chapter 8, Edward Said, professor of English Literature at Columbia University, New York; and for chapter 9, Mahfoud Bennoune, formerly a liaison officer with the Algerian National Liberation Front, now professor at the Institute of Social Science, University of Algiers.

During the three years of work on this project, we have become acquainted with Arabs of diverse backgrounds and nationalities. Throughout this book these individuals serve to illuminate the particular universe which they inhabit and which their lives describe.

We are also indebted to the series' two principal advisers, Albert Hourani of St Antony's College, Oxford University, and Martin Hinds of Trinity Hall, Cambridge University, whose expertise in the field of Middle Eastern History informs both the film series and this book.

The timely completion of a book as comprehensive as this one requires more than mere industry on the part of its contributors – it requires wit. For their wit in all senses of the word, the author would like to thank Peter Campbell, the book's designer; Angela Murphy, our picture researcher; and Carol O'Brien, the book's editor.

Finally, we wish to thank Sherry Lefevre for her invaluable help on countless fronts: research for the pictures, caption writing, text editing and general co-ordination. Without her miraculously calm and intelligent contribution, the book would never have been ready for press on time.

CHAPTER ONE

THE MAKING
OF THE
ARABS

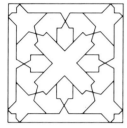

Attitudes to history vary. Superpowers, confident of their role in the world, portray their history as a steady progression to a more or less ideal present. The nation in eclipse values its past as a source of consolation; the newly independent state depends on it for precedent and legitimisation. In the case of the modern Arabs the past is especially relevant because, given the absence of something more solid, Arab identity depends inordinately on history and culture. The twentieth century has settled on one definition of national identity above all else – that of the sovereign nation-state. All citizens of the United States of America are 'Americans', and can carry the same United States passport. This common, comprehensive and *legal* American identity is never really shaken by distinctions between North and South, black and white, Catholic, Protestant or Jew, New Yorker or Texan. Not so Arab identity, even though the Arab world is less diverse, culturally and racially, than the United States. By analogy with America, the only way modern Arab identity could have been fixed in twentieth-century terms would have been for all the Arabs to form one 'United Arab States'. The excessive reliance by Arabs on a common history and culture results from the fact that they belong to twenty-one *separate* states. The fact goes a long way towards explaining why Arabs, and not only Arabs, argue so inconclusively about the nature of modern Arab identity.

Today this identity is claimed by 160 million people spread across Africa and Asia in the region of the tropic of Cancer. For want of a better term – because the Arabs are not a race, their lands are not a subcontinent and their states are not federated into a single nation – we call this phenomenon 'the Arab world'. The vague phrase is itself an admission of defeat; there is simply no appropriate noun for such an entity. Few identities intrude more frequently or more dramatically into world news yet few indeed are so poorly understood.

Arabs themselves are sufficiently uncertain about the nature of their identity to be endlessly questioning it. Not that the fact of its existence is in dispute. The two pillars of 'Arabness' – the language and culture of Arabic, and the faith of Islam – are widely acknowledged. So, too, are the burdens of the recent past and uncertain future. But

2

consensus is qualified by regional, social, economic and political factors. Egypt and Syria/Lebanon with their large Christian minorities tend to emphasise Arabic rather than Islam, language rather than religion, as the essence of Arabness; in Saudi Arabia such a distinction would be frowned on as blasphemy.

* * *

So who are the Arabs? Fifteen hundred years ago the answer would have been simple. It was in Arabia, a vast mostly arid peninsula on the margin of the great empires of the Byzantines and Persians, that a distinct identity known as 'Arab' evolved. At that time the Arabs were mostly a nomadic tribal people who took great pride in their language, revering their poets as spokesmen and acknowledging a wider identification than that of the tribe by the inclusion of other tribes who spoke the same Arabic language. In the southern part of the Peninsula, the Yemen, there was an old settled culture with close links to Ethiopia as well as contacts with Persia and Byzantium. Even in the nomadic northern part there were important permanent settlements, some engaged in agriculture, like Yathrib, and others profiting from trade up the Red Sea littoral, like the city of Mecca.

Then early in the seventh century a man living in Mecca began to teach the Quran, the Word of God revealed to him in Arabic. The Prophet Mohammed proclaimed that he was the Messenger of God's original teaching as revealed to Abraham. Now he was receiving the message in its pristine form, which would supersede the earlier holy books corrupted by the Jews and Christians in the course of time. Those who acknowledged the One God and Mohammed as His Messenger became Muslims, and the new religion was Islam. The faith revealed to Mohammed in Mecca and the society that evolved from it in Medina (formerly Yathrib) inspired and equipped the Arabs for one of the most remarkable achievements in history. It was not simply the military conquest within a century of most of the civilised world – and much of the uncivilised world – but the development of a new and distinctive civilisation unsurpassed in its day.

The Arab conquests were achieved with remarkable speed. In the 630s, within a decade of the Prophet's death, the Arab Muslim armies expelled the Byzantines from geographical Syria and the Sassanian Persians from Iraq. In a few years, this was followed in the West by the conquest of Egypt and the extension of Arab control along the coast of North Africa. In the East, the Arab armies completely replaced the Sassanian empire in Iran, and began their control of central Asia; they also conquered the Caucasus in the North. Early in the eighth century, the Arab armies conquered Spain. Thus, within a century of the rise of Islam, the Arab-Islamic empire occupied the central area of the known world; and it was a vast area. Between the cities of Cordoba in Spain and Samarkand in Central Asia there was a distance of over 4000 miles.

If you look at a map of these early Arab conquests you will notice that it covers the same area as the modern Arab world, plus Iran and Spain. In Spain most of the population remained Christian and the Christian reconquest was completed by the end of the fifteenth century. Iran was an exception; there the population converted to Islam, but in the end did not adopt Arabic.

The modern Arab world is the territory, bordered by the Atlantic ocean in the West and Iran in the East, where Arabic gradually superseded and replaced the languages used before the Arab conquests. These languages included Greek and Aramaic in Syria, Aramaic and Pahlavi in Iraq, Greek and Coptic in Egypt, Latin in North Africa. In time the majority of people in the Arab world converted to Islam, although important Christian minorities remained in geographical Syria and Egypt, and Jewish communities particularly in Iraq, North Africa and Yemen. But the triumph of the Arabic language was even greater than that of Islam, for it became the language equally of Christians and Jews. Indeed, the triumph of Arabic as the language of daily speech as well as of religion and culture is the single fact that sums up the ultimate historical consequences of the early Arab conquests for the peoples of the Arab world. This is so much the case that one can presume that without it there would be no Arab world as we know it today.

Within one generation of the death of the Prophet Mohammed, the capital of the Arab-Islamic Empire was moved to Damascus in Syria, and one century later to a newly-founded Baghdad in Iraq, near the site of ancient Babylon. It was in these ancient civilised lands, with their old cities, traditions and cultures, that the shaping of the new Arabic-Islamic civilisation took place, and from there spread to other parts of the empire. A new religion galvanised a small community on the fringes of the old world of ancient civilisations to found a state and conquer a vast empire. Within that empire, and miraculously fast, a new world civilisation was created, Arabic becoming the new dominant medium of culture and science, and Islam the religion of a vigorous and growing cosmopolitan and universal society, the heir to the ancient traditions of the Near East, of Egypt and Babylon, Greece and Persia.

The Muslims believed that the Quran is the Word of God, and gradually they evolved a great system of religious sciences based on it, the most important of which was the science of Islamic law. When Islamic higher education was institutionalised in medieval times, the colleges were primarily concerned with instruction in Islamic law. But the law, and the religious sciences generally, could not be studied without the Arabic language,

4

and philologists devoted heroic efforts to the study and systematisation of Arabic. Arabic meanwhile had absorbed the natural sciences of the Greek and other ancient traditions of the Near East, mainly through the unprecedented translation activity of the ninth century. Muslim scientists – philosophers, astronomers, mathematicians, physicians and others – continued these older national traditions and carried them further. In medieval Paris or Oxford, if you did not know the work of the Arab scientists, you were hopelessly backward. Arabic became the major scientific language of medieval times.

Politically, the Arab-Islamic empire declined very early, and by the ninth century a process of political fragmentation had started. The centralised empire of the seventh and eighth centuries gave way to independent dynasties in the provinces and governors who were practically autonomous. Power also passed from the hands of the old Arab ruling elite into those of Turkish tribesmen and others. But political fragmentation and disunity had little effect on the common Islamic-Arabic civilisation, which continued to develop with vigour, above all in the cities. In places like Fez, Cairo, Damascus and Baghdad, scholars, craftsmen and merchants preserved urban Islamic life and its institutions, and maintained continuously the links with the other cities. It is precisely in this period of endless political discord that Islamic civilisation took its mature classical form, and made its distinct contribution, in religion, literature, art and the sciences.

Contemporary Arabs view the products of classical Arabic and Islamic civilisation as their heritage. But it should be noted that this classical medieval culture is also the heritage and background of other Muslim peoples, Iranians and Turks for example. The medieval urban communities and their leaders who preserved Arab Islamic culture and created its classical forms, believed that they belonged to the one universal Muslim community, the *umma*, which was larger than the modern Arab world or modern definitions of national identity. It is this common cultural heritage, rather than a history of political unity, which is the real historical background of the Arab peoples.

*   *   *

Broadly speaking, there are four regions of the Arab world: 1, Greater Syria or 'The Fertile Crescent' includes Iraq, Syria, Jordan, Palestine and Lebanon; 2, the Nile Valley is Egypt and Sudan; 3, the Arabian peninsula includes Saudi Arabia, the Yemens and the Gulf states, and 4, the Maghreb (or 'The West') includes the present-day states of Libya, Tunisia, Algeria, Morocco and Mauritania. Each of these regions has its own historical experience, and just as the contemporary Arab world is the sum of its parts, so the contemporary Arab identity is the sum of these historical experiences.

Whether this Arab identity was coincidentally reawakened, or merely redirected by the force of changing circumstances is open to debate. But whichever it was, all are agreed that Arab nationalism as a *political* force appeared at a particular time, in a particular place, and in response to particular events. The time was 1908-14, the place was Greater Syria (especially Damascus and Beirut), and the events were those connected with the death throes of the Ottoman Empire. Throughout the nineteenth century the Ottoman Turks had been desperately trying to come to terms with the military and political superiority of the European colonial powers. In emulation of these new arrivals the Ottoman army had been reorganised, the administration decentralised, education promoted and a system of secular jurisdiction introduced. They made little difference so far as the political fate of the Ottoman Empire was concerned. The Europeans remained contemptuous, eager to assist breakaway national movements like that which led to Greek independence and eager to profit by Ottoman weakness as in North Africa, where the French and British gradually relieved the Ottomans of power.

The revolutionary activist, Jamal al-Din (1839-87), otherwise known as al-Afghani, reacted by preaching a form of pan-Islamic nationalism which emphasised the populist and revolutionary elements in Islamic tradition. His mercurial career in India, Iran, Egypt and Istanbul, with a period of exile in Paris, gave his ideas a wide currency in intellectual circles. But it was above all the style of his protest, radical, anti-authoritarian and seditious, which influenced later freedom movements. Afghani ended his days in Istanbul, a panther in chains at the court of Sultan Abd al-Hamid (1876-1908). The Sultan, like his 'protégé', believed in an Islamic revival – but one led by himself, not fermented amongst the masses. He therefore rejected constitutional reform, suspended the first Ottoman Parliament (1878) and affirmed his role as Caliph and champion of the whole Islamic world. Repressive, autocratic and erratic, Abd al-Hamid provoked as much hostility within his own Empire as he did sedition against the colonial powers outside it (in British India, Egypt and North Africa). The construction of the Hejaz railway from Damascus to Medina (1901-08) was an eye-catching achievement of which Muslims the world over approved; indeed they partly financed it. But it was also an ingenious way of tightening his grip on what remained of the Ottoman Empire, and what remained was basically an Empire of Arabs and Turks.

Resistance took two forms. Among the Syrian Arabs there was the birth of reaction against Turkish rule. According to Rashid Rida (1865-1935), the Turks were responsible for the decline of Islamic power and the only hope of renaissance lay with the Arabs. Like Abd al-Rahman al-Kawakibi (1849-1902) he was influenced by the success of the fundamentalist Wahhabi movement which had swept across Arabia in the early nineteenth century ousting, for a time, Ottoman rule even in Mecca and replacing it with a puritanical Islam. Kawakibi went so far as to dispute the Ottomans' claim to the Caliphate (or leadership of the whole world Muslim community) and to declare that only an Arab Caliph could lead a rejuvenated Islam.

Such ideas, and the men who formulated them, would shape the subsequent definitions of Arab identity. But it was not amongst disaffected Arabs but amongst the Turks themselves that dissent festered to the point of revolt. Desperate to rescue Turkish and Islamic supremacy, and resenting the fact that the Ottoman Empire was considerably more repressive than many European countries, the movement of the Young Turks spread rapidly. A coup in 1896 failed, but in 1908 mutiny succeeded. The Sultan accepted constitutional status, censorship ended, political prisoners were freed and elections held.

It looked like a miraculous recovery and was celebrated accordingly. But in the event it was no such thing. The Arabic-speaking population represented nearly half of the Empire's population; it emerged with only just over a quarter of the seats in the new parliament. The Young Turks proclaimed decentralisation and equal rights for all; after a few months of liberalisation they embarked on a policy of rigid central control and 'Turkification' of the administration and of education. Meanwhile Bosnia, Bulgaria, Libya and Crete were pared from the empire. The Young Turks responded by becoming increasingly intolerant of any pluralist talk within what remained. But Arab expectations had been aroused. Secret societies like Al-Fatat, dedicated to Arab rights within the Empire, proliferated, reform committees met, and in 1913 a Syrian Arab Congress assembled in Paris. The Turks responded by offering concessions in the matter of Arabic as the educational medium; then failed to honour them. In Beirut and Damascus the talk had been more of reform than secession, more of reviving pan-Islamic empire than breaking away from it. Language was the most divisive issue between Arabs and Turks, and in so far as the native Christian communities of Syria and Lebanon had taken the lead in dissent the fact that the language in question had Islamic connotations was not significant. But for most of the Ottoman Empire's Arabic-speaking subjects revolt was still distasteful. It would mean sundering the cherished solidarity of the Islamic community, defying established authority and cooperating with the colonial powers. It was not a decision to be taken lightly.

Yet the take-over of the Ottoman government by the Young Turks – who were secular Turkish nationalists – made it increasingly clear to a growing number of Syrian Arab Muslims that Turkish nationalism had replaced the earlier Islamic ideology of the

Empire. In reaction, Arab nationalism became the logical identification of the Syrians. Nevertheless, it was not an easy option to take, and it split many families and social groups. There is still an argument as to whether Arab nationalism in Syria before the First World War was a minority or a majority trend. In the midst of this ferment war broke out in Europe, and before the end of 1914 Turkey had joined the fray on the side of Germany. To neutralise the Turkish threat to its Middle Eastern interests, primarily in Egypt and the Suez Canal, Britain suddenly looked more favourably on the notion of independent Arab nationhood.

Thus far Arab stirrings in Syria had been more intellectual than political. But at this point the Arab world was galvanised by the success of an authentic, acceptable and richly reminiscent eruption of Arab military prowess. Hussein, the Sharif (or Governor) of Mecca and a revered descendant of the Prophet, had been held prisoner by Abd al-Hamid but had been released by the Young Turks and allowed to return to Mecca. There he had kept in touch with Arab dissent and when the Turks began executing Arab nationalists in Beirut and Damascus in 1915 he determined to act. Trusting to ambiguous British promises of support for an Arab state, in 1916 he raised the standard of revolt. Although not perhaps as romantic a campaign as T. E. Lawrence, principal British adviser with the Arab forces, would have one believe, the Arab Revolt finally transformed an intellectual protest movement into a national uprising. The tragedy was that as this transformation occurred, as Arab national identity rose to claim its place in the international world, fulfilment was denied.

The war ultimately forced them to choose between the two powerful protagonists between whom the fate of the Arab lands was being decided, the Ottoman state and the expansionist Western powers which became its heirs. In such a situation, no choice could be the right one, although many of those who finally opted for Arab independence under leadership of the Hashemites and in alliance with Britain died on the gallows in Beirut and Damascus without realising how ironically cruel the results of their choice were to be. (Rashid Khalidi)

In October 1918 the Arab forces under Hussein's son Faisal and the British forces under General Allenby entered Damascus in triumph. In due course societies such as Al Fatat came into the open, elections were held, and Faisal was elected as the constitutional king of Syria (including Lebanon and Palestine). But this arrangement was never acceptable to either Britain or France. Under the secret Sykes-Picot agreement of 1916 the colonial powers had already agreed to carve up the entire Fertile Crescent into British and French spheres of interest. The French had a long-standing interest in the Lebanon, besides ambitions to control the whole of what is now Syria. The British had their own

8

concern over the safety of the Suez Canal, of the Gulf and of Iraq's oil wealth. Furthermore they had already entered into a commitment to settle Jewish Zionists in Palestine, and this was ultimately the most fateful development of all.

The Anglo-French pact, sealed by the French storming of Damascus and destruction of Faisal's independent Arab Syrian kingdom in 1920 ('Saladin, we're back,' declared the French General standing before the tomb of the Crusaders' foe), divided the Fertile Crescent into five separate mandates. To the French went Syria and Lebanon and to the British Iraq, Transjordan and Palestine. (The installation later by the British of Faisal as king of Iraq and of his brother Abdallah as Emir of Transjordan was significant in that it could be seen as legitimising British control as well as salving British consciences; it was not a source of satisfaction for Arab nationalists.)

That the Arabs had been betrayed goes without saying. But British duplicity, French unscrupulousness, and Arab naivety are not as historically relevant as the fact that Arab identity, having been born in adversity under the Ottomans, was now robbed of its inheritance by the European democracies. If a sense of injustice and a reluctance to compromise are discernible in subsequent Arab attitudes, it is hardly surprising.

Before and during the First World War, Arab nationalism had been only a movement for Arab independence from Turkey. After the war and the division of geographical Syria, the movement began to call for reuniting the land which imperialism had so recently and artificially divided – and this is the real, or at least immediate, historical source for the idea of Arab unity (which later expanded to include much more than geographical Syria). Immediately after the war there were many problems. The Turkish military courts had executed over thirty of the best and most active nationalist leaders in Damascus and Beirut, and their talents were sorely missed in the difficult days ahead. Secondly, the new borders governed by the might of England and France effectively fragmented the Arab struggle: Iraqis were faced with the problems of the separate Iraqi mandate; Palestinians with the problem of Jewish settlement; and Syrians with a French policy that instituted even further division by creating even smaller, separate administrative units within mandate Syria.

During the inter-war years independence proved negotiable. Bombarded by strikes, boycotts, protests and uprisings, the French and British gradually withdrew from Iraq, Transjordan, Syria and Lebanon after the Second World War. But the other Arab demand – for the reunification of Greater Syria or the Fertile Crescent – was never really on the cards. At first Anglo-French rivalry precluded it; later the very fact that local independence movements were proving successful tended to perpetuate the new national entities. Each state spawned its own ruling groups and its own bureaucracy both of which had a stake in preserving independence. The arbitrary boundaries slashed across geographical Syria on imperialist maps were destined to remain. Within them, the Lebanese, Syrians, Iraqis and Jordanians were able to form their own institutions and build a new national life.

The age of European empire ended after the Second World War, and all the mandates became independent Arab states – that is, all except Palestine. In Palestine British rule, in fulfilment of the Balfour Declaration of 1917, was committed to the establishment of a Jewish homeland. This is not the place to discuss in detail the tortured history of Palestine in the twentieth century (which is the subject of Chapter Eight). But it is useful to make two points. Without the growth of Jewish settlement under the British mandate there is no reason to think that the Palestinians would have had a future much different from that of their other Arab neighbours. The second point is that the state of Israel would never have been established in Palestine had British control of Palestine not encouraged and protected Zionist immigration.

The demand for Arab unity in the 1920s and 30s applied, of course, only to Greater Syria or the Fertile Crescent. Outside this area, most of what we understand by the Arab world today was unaffected, and Arab political identity was as yet formless. Even in Cairo, which had shared in the nineteenth-century renaissance of Arabic literature and where so many Syrian intellectuals had found refuge from Ottoman censorship, the people did not regard themselves as Arabs. Or, more accurately, Egyptian identity was not expressed in Syrian-like Arab ideology. For one thing Egypt had achieved independence from Ottoman rule a century before Greater Syria, and for most of the nineteenth century the country had made rapid progress as a sovereign state in all but name. In Egypt, nationalism actually preceded colonial rule. The British could justify their occupation in 1882 on the basis of the country's strategic importance astride the route to India and on the grounds that the Egyptian treasury was about to default on its European debts. But in fact it took the popular nationalist rising of Urabi Pasha to prompt the British invasion.

The British conceded Egyptian participation in British rule, to the extent that it was never denied; but further concessions were only forthcoming under pressure. As in India, the independence movement blew hot and cold; it was practically in abeyance during the First World War. It embraced many shades of opinion – nationalist, Islamic, populist and intellectual – and pursued various strategies. As in Syria there was a demand for reunification – this time of Egypt and Sudan. But there was an obvious and important difference. In Egypt the adversary was a non-Islamic power. Religion was therefore invoked as part of the national identity, just as language was in Greater Syria. Mustafa Kamel (1874-1908), the leader of the Egyptian nationalist movement, actually combined his anti-British protest with vigorous support of the Ottoman Sultan Abd al-Hamid as leader of pan-Islam. Kamel poured scorn on the idea of an Arab Caliphate, viewing it as a colonialist plot to subvert the one remaining Ottoman Muslim state.

The inter-war years saw Egypt, like Iraq, Syria and Lebanon achieve independence. Awareness of neighbouring Arabic-speaking countries increased as Cairo, a centre of Arabic culture ever since the founding of Al-Azhar mosque university in the tenth century assumed the leadership of popular Arabic culture; the Egyptian press, radio, film and music industries crossed national frontiers which were as yet formidable barriers to any political communion. Given its geographical position at the centre of the Arabic-speaking world and its cultural and demographic pre-eminence, it was natural for Egypt to take the lead.

The British, as the price of Arab support during the Second World War, again adopted the cause of Arab unity. Under their auspices a meeting of Arab representatives took place in Alexandria in 1944, and in the following year the League of Arab States was formed. The League was a loose confederation of newly independent states – Syria, Jordan, Iraq, Lebanon and Egypt, together with Saudi Arabia and Yemen – with mutual interests which were largely economic and cultural. Concerted political action – and the involvement of Egypt in Arab political activity – came only with the emergence of a Jewish state in Palestine in the late 1940s. When the British unilaterally withdrew from Palestine in 1948, Egyptian troops joined those of the other Arab states in moving to the defence of the Palestinian Arabs. Defeat, the foundation and growing might of Israel under American tutelage, and the worsening plight of the Palestinians, would keep Egypt at the helm of Arab politics for the next twenty years. Such a powerful recruit to the cause of Arab ideology did much to sustain the frequently disappointed Syrians and Iraqis and, as the largest of the 'front-line' states, Egypt was bound to exercise a powerful role in policy-making.

This helps explain the ease with which Nasser was able to take over the leadership of the Arab world, but it does not explain the quality and charisma of his leadership. Nasser was a folk hero, a demagogue, revolutionary and reformer. By 1954 he was undisputed leader in his own country, and in 1956, the spectacle of British, French and Israeli troops ignominiously withdrawing from Suez conferred international standing on him. Through the Cairo media his defiant oratory stirred the whole Arab world – indeed the whole of the Third World. Arab political identity had become a popular force and pan-Arabism became a movement to reckon with. In 1958 the creation of the United Arab Republic of Egypt and Syria consummated these developments. Egypt had emerged as the champion of Arab identity and the pacemaker of Arab unity.

That united the Arabs were invincible had been the belief of scholars and reformers for nearly a century. Now it seemed as if the moment was ripe for the single community, like that of the early Caliphs, to re-emerge. But three short years later a military coup took Syria out of the United Arab Republic. Increasingly Nasser devoted his energies to social and economic reform although pan-Arabism continued as a political force until the Seven Day War of 1967. Even after that catastrophe Nasser remained a popular hero. But subsequent declarations of unification – such as that between Egypt and Libya – carried little conviction.

After 1967, and especially after 1973 and the rise in the price and importance of oil, attention shifted to the Arabian Peninsula as the most important region of the Arab world. This was a new development. When the rest of the Arab world was entering the modern age and wrestling with the challenge of Western Europe, the fact that Arabia remained desperately poor, undeveloped and untouched by the outside world did not diminish its importance. Mecca had continued to be the great forum of the Islamic and Arab world thanks to the Muslim obligation of pilgrimage. But in the more secular climate of today, when the mass media have to some extent usurped Mecca's role as a point of cultural exchange, and when nationalism and socialism have eroded the role of religion, Arabia might have seemed destined to lose its hold on the Arab consciousness. That it has not, that more than ever Arabia is the focus of Arab attention, that more Arabs than ever spend more time there than ever, is mostly due to oil. In a couple of decades one of the world's poorest, most backward and most politically insignificant countries has become one of the richest and most influential. In Kuwait, the Gulf Emirates and Riyadh new concepts of Arab cooperation are evolving, new problems are being tackled, and new hopes are being born. But all this is happening in what is still an intensely conservative and traditional part of the Arab world.

Yet it is impossible to understand the development of Arabia and the Gulf in isolation from the rest of the Arab world. Only thirty years ago, for instance, Kuwait was a poor, underpopulated settlement. Today it has become a thriving, modernising and dynamic city-state, a central modern Arab city. It did not achieve this simply by an independent 'telescoping' of a hundred-year-old modern Arab experience in education, politics, bureaucracy, science, the modern Arabic language and outlook. Instead it acquired and internalised Arab experience by attracting other Arabs to itself. As employees, scientists, professors and journalists, Egyptians, Palestinians and Lebanese live and work in Kuwait.

There is no issue discussed anywhere in the Arab world that is not discussed publicly, one way or another, in Kuwait. There was a time when only the press of Beirut came close to being a truly Arab-wide press; it is possible to argue now that the newspapers published in Kuwait come closest. They are larger, better edited, and show a degree of freedom unmatched by publications in any other Arab country. All of them write explicitly as if their audience consisted of all the Arabs.

'Islam is our religion, Arabic our language, Algeria our country,' chant the children at morning assembly in every Algerian state school. At home their parents may speak Berber and in the common room their teachers may still lapse into French. But the language of the new generation is Arabic. In 1962 when the country finally won independence it was in a state of acute cultural denudation. A hundred years of colonisation had established French as the medium of government, education, advancement and culture with Arabic being relegated to the status of an intellectual discipline pursued by a handful of intellectuals. But (as is described in Chapter Nine) the sudden departure of nearly a million French settlers meant the loss of this entire cultural topsoil. There was a real crisis of identity – one to which the government responded with a policy of vigorous Arabisation. 11% of the gross national product was devoted to education, schools built, teachers and textbooks imported and by 1974 all primary and secondary education was in Arabic and basic schooling had been extended to the entire population.

A similar policy of Arabisation has been going on in the other countries of the Maghreb; and educational expansion is a feature of the entire Arab world. Without either conquest or conversion the number of people sharing an Arab identity is today growing faster even than during the period of Arab expansion in the seventh to ninth centuries. Emphatically it is not just a question of speaking Arabic but of participating in Arab culture. School textbooks in Algeria are printed in Arabic and they are Arab textbooks, the same as those used by Kuwaiti and Jordanian children. Through Arabic, students acquire a common set of historical and cultural references, and intellectuals share in one Arab cultural community.

This cultural fluidity, which applies to publishing, the media and the arts as well as to scholarship, has always been a feature of the Arab-Islamic world. But today the scale and penetration of such interchange is wholly unprecedented. What it may forbode in political and economic terms is anyone's guess; the Maghrebi component in the sum of Arab historical awareness lies in a future that is imponderable but imminent.

If Arabs today agree on anything it is that they have little cause for self-congratulation. The chance of political unity was squandered, and even concerted action has been sacrificed for economic, ideological and party advantage. But this chapter of defeats masks what many Arabs believe may yet prove to be a very significant victory. Arabhood exists quite apart from its national and political connotations. Political uncertainty is being matched by a remarkable diffusion of Arab cultural identity.

13

1. Shibam in the Hadhramaut, the People's Democratic Republic of Yemen. Despite their modern appearance, houses like these have been built for over a thousand years.

Today, as always, the Arab world is city orientated. Islam was first adopted by the city-dwellers of Medina and Mecca; its laws and institutions were formulated in an urban context; and the Arab conquests of the seventh and eighth centuries resulted in an empire of glittering cities. Many of them, like the Abbasid capital of Baghdad, were founded by the Arabs.

2. *Port Said, Egypt*

3. *Al-Chebayish on the Tigris and Euphrates in Iraq*

4. *Dubai, the United Arab Emirates*

5. Jeddah, Saudi Arabia

The inequalities of economic wealth and the contrasts of colonialism and independence are reflected in the architecture and social environment of today's Arabs. In the Middle Ages the Arab world was the closest thing to a universal civilisation that the world has ever seen. Diversity was offset by a uniformity in social, intellectual and religious life which transcended even dynastic and political divisions.

6. A Berber sheep market in the Middle Atlas Mountains, Morocco

Extending from the Atlantic to the Gulf and from sub-tropical Africa to the mountains of Anatolia, the Arab world comprehends extremes c
climate and terrain. The desert tribesman is as unrepresentative of the Arabs as a whole as the Nile peasant or the North African wine grower. I
a civilisation traditionally based on great cities, the rural environment may give an unreliable impression of regional particularism.

7. Oil fields in Libya

8. The Sebka Valley
in the Sahara Desert,
Algeria

9. The Empty
Quarter, Saudi
Arabia

10. *In the suburbs of Cairo, Egypt*

11. *Bait al Faqih in the Tihara Plain of the Yemen Arab Republic*

12. (top left) Schoolchildren in Umduban, Sudan   13. (top right) Berber girl   14. (bottom left) Factory workers in Jordan   15. (bottom right) Tuaregs in Algeria
Facing page: 16. Ex-soldier, now a farmer in Saudi Arabia

All Arabs speak a common language, acknowledge a predominant religion, and revere a shared past. They are not a race; people of negro, Berber and semitic origin acknowledge an Arab identity. Neither are they a nation-state, although the call of Arab unity strikes a sympathetic chord. Arab identity now transcends diversities of nationality and ideology as traditionally it has those of race and region.

CHAPTER TWO

THE POWER
OF THE
WORD

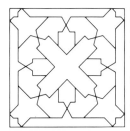 In February 1983 the Palestinian Liberation Organisation was holding a congress in Algeria. Delegates from all over the Arab world and beyond, in fact from wherever PLO men had found sanctuary following the 1982 exodus from Beirut, converged on Algiers. Amongst them was Yasser Arafat. His leadership seemed under threat and with it any chance of a negotiated settlement of the Palestine issue. In fact the threat did not materialise. But there was a scare.

Late one night after hours of speech making, the fog of revolutionary rhetoric lifted, briefly. Arafat suddenly rushed out of the hall, his bodyguards jogging beside him, and tore away in a motorcade. Rumours flew that he had resigned.

The truth was more extraordinary. The world's most famous guerrilla leader had gone to fetch a poet. He returned holding the hand of Mahmoud Darwish who began at midnight to declaim his latest poem, on the battle of Beirut. It went on until 2 a.m. The hundreds of delegates listened with rapt attention.

Arafat stared at Darwish with almost childlike adoration. When after the final stanza Darwish slumped exhausted into his chair, Arafat went to the microphone and spoke a little poem of his own. 'The revolution is not just guns; it is the pen of the poet, the needle of the woman who makes scarves for the fighters.' He sat down to thunderous applause. (*Sunday Times, 27 February 1983*)

Fifteen hundred years ago the Arab tribes of the Arabian peninsula held their poets in equal regard. In harsh nomadic conditions, unfavourable to arts like painting and sculpture, language was cherished as the supreme medium of creative expression. The poet was the soul of the tribe; he was also its mouthpiece, its propagandist and its chronicler. He spoke for all his people, expressing their communal pride and longings. As such he embodied the collective unity of his people; he was parliament and public opinion. There was also wizardry in his words and he could conjure such images out of the empty desert as made warriors quake and chiefs defer to him. The Prophet himself would be wary of these poets and feel constrained to condemn their bewitching powers, enlisting his devoted follower, the poet Hassan Ibn Thabit, to recite in his defence.

Although writing was not unknown to the pre-Islamic Arabs few of these poems were written down at the time. They were composed, sung and memorised at tribal gatherings and at great poetry contests. The language had to be memorable, formal but rich in resonance and rhyme, the imagery subtle and fanciful but always concrete. Tribal maidens are seen to wheel and shy like gazelles; sorrow is as bitter as the colocynth; and the old man who, tired of moving on, huddles down in each new encampment, is like that sluggish last drop of milk that stays in the camel's teat after milking. Never has animal been laden with a greater burden of metaphor than the long-suffering Arabian camel.

The most famous anthology of these poems is the *Mu'allaqat*, a collection of seven long odes by different poets who were committed to writing in the Islamic period. They speak of love and battle, of tribal honour and personal valour, of the comforts of society and the plight of alienation, of endless journeying and of the mystery of the desert. Recognising the formidable difficulties of an exact translation Sir William Jones, the great eighteenth-century orientalist, strove simply to evoke something of the visionary spirit of the original.

> The cloud unloads its freight on the desert of Ghabeit,
> 　like a merchant of Yemen alighting with his bales or rich apparel.
> The small birds of the valley warble at daybreak,
> 　as if they had taken their early draught of generous wine mixed with spice.
> The beasts of the wood, drowned in the floods of night,
> 　float, like the roots of wild onions, at the distant edge of the lake.

A common tendency towards boasting propaganda was tempered by an overwhelming nostalgia at the impermanence of life. Pastures wither, wells dry up, beauty fades, loved ones depart. A recurrent theme is that of the forlorn camp site rich in the memories of youth and plenty, but now abandoned to the encroachment of a sandy oblivion. Poetry alone defies change, preserves and immortalises. So long as there is a poet there is a people. And so long as there is a poet there will be a Palestine. Mahmoud Darwish, not Yasser Arafat, embodies the PLO.

To a people already susceptible to the word came The Word. The first lines of divine revelation, as vouchsafed to the Prophet in a cave near Mecca, are significant.

> Recite: In the name of thy Lord who created,
> 　created Man of a blood-clot.
> Recite: And thy Lord is the Most Generous
> 　who taught by the Pen
> 　taught Man what he knew not.

Quran means 'Recitation', the Recitation of God's plan for mankind. To listen to the Quran, to learn it by heart and to recite it (without necessarily grappling with its meaning) is in itself highly meritorious. According to the Traditions of the Prophet (hadith), 'the best act of worship [that may be performed by] my community is the recitation of the Quran. The best among you is he who learns and teaches the Quran. The people of God and his favourites are those of the Quran.' When reciting, such things as pronunciation, diction and intonation must be perfect. For the Quran is, literally, the Word of God, its revelation through the Prophet and its codification by his successors: a miraculous process. It must therefore be handled with the utmost reverence. The very words have a power which, because of their divine composition, reaches directly into the hearts of men. By the same reasoning they partake of divine perfection in being unassailably beautiful and correct, beyond the pale of literary criticism.

Insofar as Arabic now had an exemplar of perfection that was good for all time, it was inevitable that the grammar, vocabulary and syntax used in the Quran should be accepted as the purest of their kind. Subsequently a formidable weight of scholarship would be brought to bear on Quranic interpretation and on the numerous branches of philology. And here a need emerged constantly to refer back to the past, in this case to the age of early Islam when the language was supposedly unsullied by foreign accretions, as pure as the desert whence it came.

The very structure of Arabic words provides an analogy of this process. Words with related meanings are usually derived from a simple root of three consonants. Thus k-t-b gives *kitab*, a book, *kataba*, to write, *katib*, an author, *katibah*, an authoress, *kitabah*, script, *kuttab*, a school, *kutubi*, bookseller, *maktab*, office, *mukatabah*, correspondence, *maktabah*, bookshop and so on. The possibilities seem endless and indeed the beauty of this system was that, up to a point, Arabic could absorb new forms and allocate them meanings with existing word-forms.

This system and the further elaboration of each word-form according to the rules of syntax also gives a clue to the highly allusive quality of the language and to its rhyme and rhythm. Distinctions as between prose and rhetoric, or between prose and poetry, can never be as clear-cut in Arabic as, say, in English. For instance, the celebrated ninth- and tenth-century *Maqamat*, social sketches, of al-Hamadhani and al-Hariri are described as prose but are in fact rhyming prose. The power of the word is thus all-pervasive, heightening the effect of the language even as it enhances its clarity.

Something similar is true of the Arabic script. The image of the word, like its sound, transcends mere meaning; writing becomes calligraphy, an art based on strict formal canons but capable of extraordinary refinement, elaboration and expression. A glance at a page of Arabic calligraphy immediately suggests some exceptionally elegant form of musical notation; and in its visual appeal it hints at a further analogy for the resonant and harmonious possibilities of the language. Just a dozen basic shapes, differentiated by dots below and above, give a 28-letter alphabet. But with most of these letters having a different form depending on whether it falls at the beginning, middle or end of a word, each word itself takes on a harmonious unity, and the same is true of each line and of each page. In any of the several different calligraphic scripts – from the early angular *kufi* to the simple *ruq'ah* of everyday writing to the elaborate *diwani* – the proportions of each letter are based on the module of the *alif*, or long 'a'. Thus basic visual rhythms are established which the artist can perfect, elaborate and exaggerate to achieve artistic effect.

The elevation of calligraphy to the status of fine art and its importance in architecture as well as literature was connected with the Islamic suspicion of figurative and representational art. If depictions of the human form were to be avoided, abstract art and, in particular, the arabesque and writing, might be expected to emerge as the main form of visual expression. But early Islam was also much influenced by Judaic thought and, of course, openly claimed to be the true and original religion of Abraham. The Jewish prohibition of graven images was thus inherited by Islam. Moreover, the expansion of Islam happened to coincide with a period when even Byzantine Christianity was having serious doubts about the propriety of religious images.

The Quran says nothing about figurative art, apart from forbidding the worship of idols, and from the remarkable frescoes in the Umayyad palace at Qusayr Amrah in Jordan it is clear that the human figure was acceptable in the eighth century, at least in secular contexts. Other frescoes in the Umayyad mosque in Damascus depict trees and lakes in architectural settings, the conventional backgrounds for Byzantine art, although without the central figure or icon. But at about the time that Eastern Christians reverted to the idea of images, Islam proscribed them, and the prohibition on figurative art is evident in the later religious literature. Christian reasoning was based on the doctrine of salvation. If the Son of God came down to earth in human form then surely it was legitimate to portray Him in human form. But the same argument did not hold good for Muslims. In Islam the Word was emphatically *not* made flesh. It remained the Word and while Christians might concentrate on the imitation of Christ, Muslims must model their lives on the Law as laid down by the Word, the Holy Quran.

When conquest brought the Arabs into closer contact with the sophisticated cultures of Sassanian Persia and of Greek Byzantium, they were impressed and influenced. But the Arab newcomers retained their conviction of superiority and invoked the Quran as apologia, propaganda and art. The Word as Art – it was an exciting idea and one for which the Arabic script was perfectly suited. If the muezzin climbed the minaret to summon the faithful to prayer through the spoken word then why not incorporate suitable verses of the written word into the architecture of the mosque? The first known examples of Quranic inscriptions being used in architecture are found in the Dome of the Rock in Jerusalem (AD 691). In that the verses chosen address themselves to the 'people of the Book' (i.e. Jews and Christians), they help explain the existence and purpose of this otherwise puzzling building. It would seem that its builder, the Caliph Abd al-Malik, had in mind a statement of having, as it were, 'arrived' – a hoisting of the Islamic flag above those of Christendom and Israel in the holiest of cities and on a spot closely associated with Abraham (Ibrahim of the Quran). In this context the profession of Islamic faith, which is included in the original inscriptions, becomes a resounding and triumphant expression of the universality of God. The verse proclaims the triumph of Islam and the calligraphy proclaims the triumph of the Word.

> God bears witness that
> there is no God but He –
> and the angels, and the men possessed of knowledge –
> upholding justice;
> there is no God but He,
> the All-mighty, the All-wise.
> The true religion with God is Islam.

*   *   *

The evolution of Arabic as a universal language with enormous religious and cultural importance has been acknowledged as 'the true wonder of Arab expansion'. It was one thing for Arab armies to sweep across Mesopotamia and Persia, North Africa and Spain but quite another for them to impose their comparatively basic desert language on subject but highly developed cultures. Ultimately, this became possible by reason of the development of Arabic as an effective and precise instrument of culture and science. Although all these things were happening simultaneously there was some element of cause and effect. At first the Arabs used the local languages – Syriac, Aramaic, Pahlavi, Greek, Coptic and Latin – for administrative purposes just as they used Byzantine mosaicists, painters and architects for their buildings. The speed of conquest had temporarily outstripped the pace of cultural evolution and shown up the inadequacies of the Arabic language in, for instance, expressing concepts essential to the government of large settled populations. But this imbalance was short-lived. The Arab's attachment to his language and religion, his conviction of their superiority and universality, never wavered. After the armies of conquest had moved east and west an army of scholars was set to work codifying grammar and syntax, elaborating the laws of word formation and standardising the script.

So long as Arabic rose to each new challenge and so long as it remained the language of the ruling elite and of their religion, a process of spontaneous acculturation amongst the subject peoples was inevitable. An almost exact, but better documented, parallel is found in the extension of British rule in India in the late eighteenth and early nineteenth centuries. There too the sudden acquisition of vast territories with their own legal, fiscal and administrative customs posed a challenge which was met by a period of Indianisation when the British adopted Urdu or Bengali as the appropriate languages of government. And there too the experiment was short-lived. English remained the language of the ruling elite and as the British sense of superiority – more moral and technological in this case, but spurred on by the Evangelical movement – reasserted itself, so too did the belief in Anglicisation. English never quite achieved the same level of cultural penetration as did Arabic, but insofar as it remains the language of government and scholarship in India, it is not far short of the Arabic component in the Maghreb prior to colonial interference and the nationalist awakening.

Two other important aspects of Arab expansion are relevant: expansion entailed a transition from the desert to the city – from camp to court; and it was marred by outbreaks of dynastic and religious dissension. Both had an inspirational effect on Arabic as a literary language.

It has often been remarked that the latitudinal sprawl of the Arab world is proof that Arab rule flourished only in arid, if not desert, regions and eschewed the moist tropics to the south and the cold wooded pastures to the north. This was not simply a question of preference but had to do with the contemporary political balance and with the nature of Arab military tactics. But the phenomenon could equally well be explained in terms of the success of Arab rule in city-based societies. Before and after the Arab conquests power, trade and scholarship in all these regions were concentrated in the cities, thus simplifying the process of Arabisation. The Arabs also built their own cities and showed a predilection for city life. Mecca and Medina were flourishing centres even before Islam; the Prophet himself was a Meccan merchant and Islam first took hold not amongst nomadic tribes but amongst the comparatively sophisticated city dwellers of Medina. The notion of tribal solidarity had been easily transformed into that of urban solidarity and that of Islamic solidarity.

At the same time the success of Arab arms meant a steady flow of plunder and taxes back to the cities. In Mecca and Medina, then Damascus and Baghdad, a wealthy and discriminating aristocracy grew up around the Caliphate and under its patronage the traditions of secular poetry revived. A flourishing genre of *ghazal*, or romantic, poetry developed from the lovelorn preludes of the *Mu'allaqat*. Melancholic to the point of spirituality, or brazenly erotic, these poems were often recited to music, the metre being shortened and the language simplified. So provocative were the mischievous amours related by Umar bin Abi Rabi'ah of Mecca that the pious blushed at his verses, but not all of them refrained from memorising them.

By way of contrast the political role of the pre-Islamic bard was also reinstated. Poets won over to Islam extolled the virtues of the new faith and its leaders, and when the Caliphate was in dispute each of the contending parties had its poetic spokesman. So too did religious dissenters like the Shi'ites and the Kharijites. Poetry remained at the centre of political affairs, an immensely powerful method of rallying support and of disheartening the opposition. At the celebrated contests, poets, locked in gladiatorial combat, hurled metrical invective at one another. Mastery of the Arabic language was deemed so essential to office that prospective Caliphs as well as philologists and grammarians repaired to the deserts of Arabia to perfect their techniques at source.

As a knowledge of Arabic and of the Quran became increasingly desirable to non-Arabs, so the codification of the language and the standardisation of the script made it more accessible. By the late eighth century Arabic was well on the way to the status of a universal language spoken and written by the intelligentsia from Central Asia to Spain. The strain of such dramatic acculturation showed in the demands now made on the language. Fables from India, philosophical and scientific works from ancient Greece, and prose traditions from Persia, were all gathered within the fold of Arabic literature. Whether it was a case of straight translation, of re-creation, or purely of inspiration, Arabic was enriched with new words, new ideas and new genres. The Abbasid period (from the eighth to the thirteenth centuries), the golden age of Arab-Islamic culture, was marked by the heroic endeavour of grammarians and lexicographers to preserve the purity of the language whilst broadening its capabilities.

It was also a period of ferocious controversy with modernists embracing the new climate and devising simpler or more popular styles while the neo-classicists turned away in disgust to seek inspiration in the pre-Islamic odes. Both modernists and neo-classicists continued to champion the interests of their patrons and to participate in political debate. The role of the poet, his themes – love, wine, religion, politics, society – and his repertoire of poetic forms remained much the same. But there was an increasing obsession with verbal virtuosity and with the elaboration of imagery. As an example of this, Professor A. J. Arberry quotes two short verses of the thirteenth-century

Andalusian poet Ibn al-Sabuni and then shows how every image – that is nearly every word – is rich in associations to anyone familiar with Arabic.

> She is coming, coming,
> So soft her tread,
> A moon in gloaming
> Rose garmented.
>
> As if her glances
> My lifeblood shed,
> And wiped their lances
> In her robe of red.

In the later Middle Ages, modernism was characterised by this precious refinement of language and imagery whilst neo-classicism went in for excessive intellectualisation. But, by way of contrast, a genre of folk verse couched in the colloquial dialects of Arabic and with a strong narrative appeal continued to flourish. The oral traditions of the pre-Islamic bard had never in fact died and, to delight the illiterate masses, stories of Antarah, a pre-Islamic hero, continued to be told in the villages and along the caravan routes. Antarah was one of the underprivileged and a negro; so was Abu Zayd leader of the Bani Hilal tribe. Their sagas are still told by itinerant story-tellers in North Africa and performed in shadow theatres in the coffee houses of Damascus.

Also belonging to this colloquial tradition is the collection of popular stories gathered together from a variety of sources under the title of *Alf Laylah wa Laylah – The Thousand and One Nights*. Rather as today the Third World has appropriated one particular genre of Western music (Rock and Roll) as typical of Western civilisation, so Europeans of the eighteenth and nineteenth centuries appropriated the 'Arabian Nights', (including Ali Baba, Aladdin and Sinbad) as representative of Arab-Islamic culture. Classical Arabic literature, like classical Western music, was largely ignored with the result that in each case oversimplification, characterised by grotesque stereotypes, prejudiced genuine cultural interaction. But if this popular genre was largely irrelevant to classical Arabic *belles lettres*, its survival into the twentieth century was important.

*   *   *

'The main question is that of identity. But what I mean by identity is not merely to be Arab. Of course all of us are Arab. No question. No problem about it. The question is what do we represent? What are our hopes? What do we want to do? What do we want to express? . . . We are looking to the past, to the roots. We are looking to the future. We are looking to the West. But all the time we are putting questions. Arab poetry is mainly a poetry of repudiation. It's a poetry of questioning.'

Khalida Said, literary critic and wife of the *avant-garde* poet Adonis, cries as she speaks. She is tired; Beirut, their home, and Lebanon, their country, are being savagely dismembered around them; and an interviewer is quizzing her about Arabic literature.

'Beirut for me is the physical picture of Arabic culture today. Here in Beirut everything is crumbling. Yet life is there; everything is going to be born again. I can see it like a terrible vision but I can see the new life surging from it. In the West you have plenty of answers, plenty of theories. We don't have theories. We have mainly questions. Because we are not sure. We are not sure of anything now. We are searching. We are looking for this dynamic . . .'

Many would dispute the idea that in 1982 the war-sundered city of Beirut symbolised the state of contemporary Arabic literature. They would agree that literature faithfully mirrors the turmoil, uncertainties and hopes of the Arab world, but they would not necessarily acknowledge Beirut's plight as being representative of it. This, however, is Khalida's point. The great paradox of Arab culture – now more than ever – is that whilst the common language and heritage of Arabic confer a veneer of unity and identity, the same factors – language and heritage – bequeath a legacy of particularism. The poet speaks for his tribe, his princely patron, his nation; but who speaks for all the Arabs? Khalida weeps over the spectacle of disarray. And she clings to the belief in a new 'dynamic' which will end conflict and compel the Arabs – and indeed the whole world – to acknowledge Beirut, to acknowledge their responsibility, their involvement, their common identity.

The renaissance of Arabic literature began in the late nineteenth century and has paralleled the growth of Arab nationalism, inspiring it, sustaining it, hymning it and mourning it to this day. But there is another, less probable, parallel with the classical Abbasid period. Just as the introduction of paper from China in the eighth century was highly significant for the dissemination of classical literature, so the proliferation of the printing press in Egypt and Syria during the mid-nineteenth century was inseparable from the renaissance. And just as the poets of the classical period divided into neo-classicists and modernists, so the renaissance had its own neo-classicists and modernists. The former revived the traditions of correct Arabic and refined style. They encouraged the swell of nationalism by emphasising the glories of the past and by arousing latent aesthetic sensibilities. The modernists delved into the culture of the West. At first there were straight translations of Western works, then Arabic versions of them, then creative writing in Arabic exploiting typically modern themes such as social comment, personal experience and psychological exploration. The short story and the novel, grafted on to the prose traditions of the *Maqamat* and the narrative traditions of the popular story-teller, were welcomed as acceptable literary forms and soon enjoyed great popularity. Likewise the theatre which was unknown in the Arab world before the nineteenth century.

The cornucopia of Western culture seemed inexhaustible. Backed by the might of colonialism and enhanced by the dazzle of modernity, Western ideas in law, politics, economics and science were stockpiled at the gates of Arabic translation. The old problem of how Arabic – or any classical language for that matter – could absorb such an array of novel and alien concepts and still retain its authenticity and concision became critical. Theoretically the coining of new scientific and technical terms should present no problem. Rules for creating new words – by derivation from existing roots, by using Arabic metaphors or simply Arabising foreign words – were established in the Middle Ages. The trouble is that in spite of numerous commissions, programmes and conferences, no uniform standard has been adopted. While the debate grows ever more heated each part of the Arab world, each centre of learning, each separate discipline finds its own solutions. The result is often a confusing multiplicity of words all meaning the same thing. There is no doubt that this is a greater problem than the need to reform the Arabic script, though the need for simplification of the script has been widely acknowledged. The system of designating vowel sounds can be highly confusing and there are too many variations of each letter form. But the idea of romanising the script, as Ataturk did in Turkey, did not gain ground. The script, like the language, is sacrosanct in the eyes of the devout and no less precious in the eyes of the secular nationalist. It is one of the most obvious links with the past and one of the most distinctive signs of Arab identity.

It is this concern with identity that has led contemporary Arab writers to ask, in the words of Khalida Said, 'How can we share seriously and deeply with world culture, and remain authentic?' To live in the world today and also remain authentic has led many contemporary artists back to their own heritage, not as a refuge, but as a point of departure. This return has to some extent defused what some had regarded as a potentially explosive confrontation between literary Arabic and the numerous colloquial dialects. In everyday life most Arabs speak a colloquial dialect which may be incomprehensible to other Arabs but which is nevertheless the authentic and expressive idiom of the people. Writers of fiction have often seen the colloquial dialect as the only appropriate means of expression in an egalitarian society. And in the theatre the rejection of classical (in this case Western) forms has been taken to its logical extreme by *avant-garde* directors like Roger Assaf who improvises his pavement dramas using not only colloquial speech but random anecdote. It is all part of the process of tracing art back to its roots in life, an ideal as dear to the Arab socialist as that of tracing culture to its roots in the past is to the Arab nationalist.

But literary Arabic remains supreme, not just because of its religious and cultural associations, but because it has found a powerful champion in the mass media. The most influential newspapers, like Cairo's *Al-Ahram*, were founded during the nationalist awakening in the late nineteenth century. Language was the platform of proto-nationalism and a modernised version of classical Arabic was adopted, which is now used by the entire Arab press, radio and television for all news dissemination and much else besides. A Nasser speech may have lapsed into the Egyptian vernacular but the transcript in the papers was entirely in the literary Arabic. The media are in fact promoting Arabic as successfully as the Quran did a millennium ago. The Arabs, like the modern Greeks, are learning to live with a formal written language that is not the same as the spoken dialect.

But even printed, the word has explosive potential. So long as a book or a newspaper printed anywhere in the Arab world is intelligible to all Arabs, the cultural component of pan-Arabism will remain a formidable force. In the early years of Arab nationalism, Cairo was the publishing centre and in terms of popular culture – films, music, television and radio – it retains its pre-eminence (with the significant consequence that the Egyptian Arabic colloquial dialect is now understood by Arabs everywhere, from Morocco to the Gulf). Recently other cities, like Baghdad or Kuwait, have also made their mark as publishing centres. But for most of this century the Fleet Street and the Bloomsbury of the Arab world have been located in Beirut. As an intellectual capital Beirut was ideal. Traditionally outward-looking, highly literate and politically liberal, Lebanon offered the perfect climate for the germination and propagation of ideas. Beirut became a free port for intellectual and artistic exchange. With six universities, hundreds of publishing houses and more newspapers than anywhere else in the Arab world, it could claim to be the mouthpiece of the Arabs. When Khalida Said cites the now ruined city as evidence of the plight of Arabic culture she may simply be stating the obvious. Whither literature without publishers? Whither Arabic without Beirut?

But in reality it is, of course, more than that: 'Because literature is not merely literature. For us it is the expression of this historical moment, these Arab sufferings, strugglings, searchings. Literature is not just beautiful words for us. The audience cannot get mad just over beautiful words. Poetry here is the hurt expression, the hurt, the beautiful and authentic expression of this special moment. It is the open heart of the Arab world.'

The power of the word is still epitomised by the poet. In 1898 the Egyptian Ahmad Shauqi listed the credentials of the modern Arabic poet. 'Firstly he must have the conviction that poetry is part of his nature; secondly he must have both learning and experience; and lastly poetry should not be a frill in his life but an enduring occupation.' In 1971 Abd al-Wahab al Bayyati, an Iraqi, divided the poet's essential vision into three very different components, 'an objective understanding of the paradoxes of existence, a discovery of the logic of history, and a dynamic involvement in the events of his own time.' Shauqi was a modernist, al-Bayyati a Marxist. Between their extremes of artistic integrity and activist commitment every possible nuance of attitude is represented by contemporary Arab poets. From classical metre to free verse and from Islamic piety to social realism they have run the gamut of forms and themes. But their work must still be put to the test in a public recital. And its ability to rouse the audience will still depend on the poet's facility in exploiting the power and beauty of the Arabic language itself.

As Khalida Said bemoans the ruins of Beirut, her husband, Adonis, intones his elegy for the city, in the voice of the *New Noah*:

> Oh, we wish we hadn't become seed
> for the earth
> for its generations.
> We wish we had remained clay
> so as not to see the world
> so as not to see
> its hell and god twice.

One is reminded of that overpowering sense of melancholy which typified the Arabian bard's lament over a deserted encampment. However fanciful, there is a parallel between the plight of today's Arabs and that of the pre-Islamic tribes – both searching the horizon for a new dynamic but surrounded by the evidence of past failures, both politically divided but united in language and culture, both proud and unsettled, both addicted to poetry and acknowledging an identity based on the word. The past does not always have to be evoked; sometimes it repeats itself.

> Halt, friends both! Let us weep, recalling a love and a longing
> by the rim of the twisted sands between Ed-Dakhool and Haumal,
> Toodih and El-Mikrat, whose trace is not yet effaced
> for all the spinning of the south winds and the northern blasts;
> there, all about its yards, and away in the dry hollows
> you may see the dung of antelopes spattered like peppercorns.
> Upon the morn of separation, the day they loaded to part,

by the tribe's acacias it was like I was splitting a colocynth;
there my companions halted their beasts awhile over me
saying, 'Don't perish of sorrow; restrain yourself decently!'
Yet the true and only cure of my grief is tears outpoured;
what is there left to lean on where the trace is obliterated?

(From the *Mu'allaqat*: 'The Ode of Imru'al-Qays' translated by Arberry)

1. A young boy practises writing the Quran in the 'madrassah' of the Al Djanad Mosque in the Yemen Arab Republic

Spoken or written the Word has a power which transcends meaning. Quran means 'Recitation' and the Quran declares that 'God taught by the pen'. Learning the Word of God by correct recitation and accurate copying is the basis of traditional education. Thus does a child first learn to read and write.

2. *Spanish Book of Prayer, 13th century*

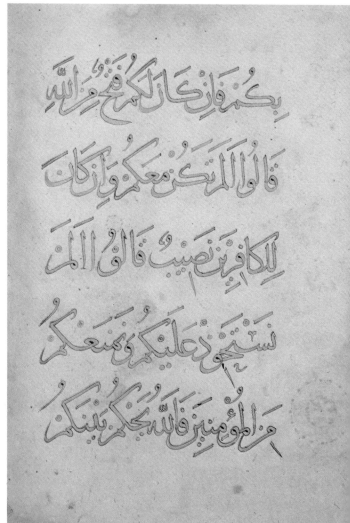

3. *Baghdad Quran, 13th century*

Historically the evolution of Arabic as a written language coincided with the birth and propagation of Islam. Calligraphic styles developed in the early centres of Arab-Islamic culture – Mecca, Medina, Basra and Kufa – but it was Kufic alone which in the late eighth century became established as the principal script for Quranic calligraphy. From it developed the lighter 'bent' Kufic (4) and the popular Nashki (3). In the West a rounding of the angles and an exaggeration of the sub-linear curves heralded the development of the elegant Maghrebi (2) which spread from tenth-century Tunisia throughout North Africa and Muslim Spain.

4. *Eastern Quran, 10th century*

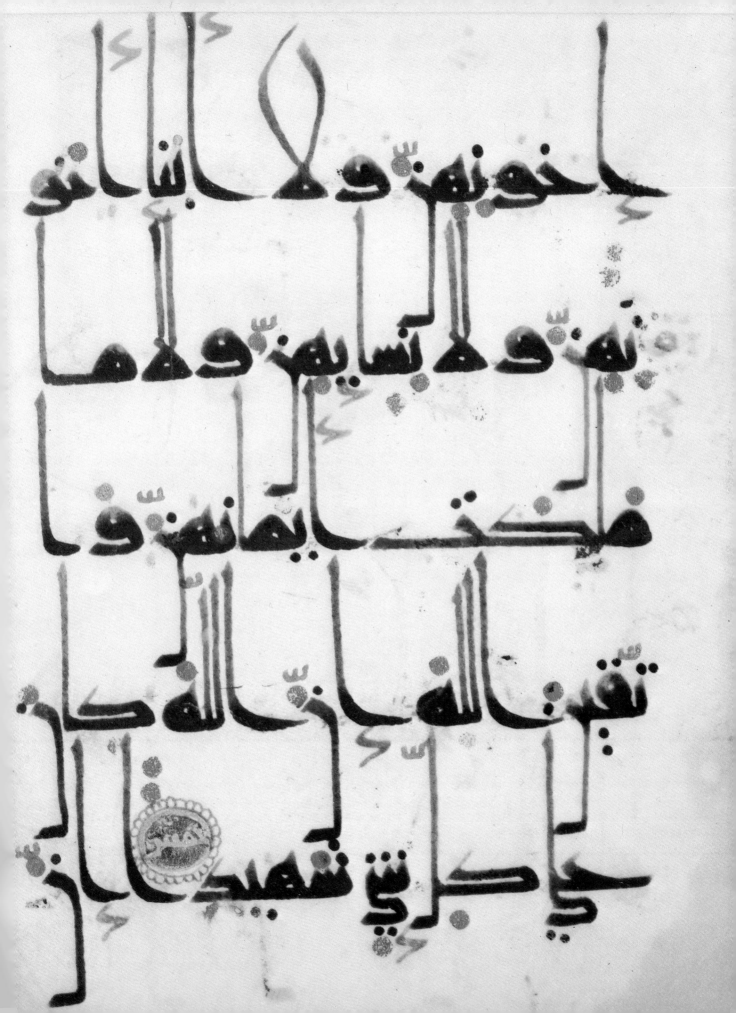

5. Once again the roguish Abu Zayd meets up by chance with al-Harith and his group who are listening to a fellow singer in a suburb of Baghdad. With his usual penchant for word-play he challenges them with some of his riddles

In the 'Maqamat' al-Hariri (born 1054), a protégé of the Abbasid court in Baghdad, used a rhyming prose of consummate ingenuity to relate the picaresque encounters of his narrators with the ubiquitous Abu Zayd. These amusing anecdotes became classics in the author's lifetime and even in Andalusia were part of the literary curriculum. Widely imitated and translated, they reached Europe through a Latin translation in the seventeenth century. Though revered for their literary virtuosity, they were also notable for the spirited illustrations by al-Wasiti which convey a vivid picture of social life in the twelfth century.

6. The author locates this scene in the public library of his own native city, Basra. Throughout the 8th and 9th centuries Basra in Iraq was the home of intense religious and intellectual activity. The fame of its library endured long after Basra had receded into the shadow of Baghdad and provides an appropriate setting for al-Harith's discussion of literary topics with a group of writers

فقال إمام الله للحق أجوز أن ينبع وللصدق وحقين أن ينبع إنه أقوم لبحكم وللذليوم وألا فكان الجماعة

إن أبن عروة وأبن نصرو يدعوننه فنوحس ما هجن فنوحس في أفكارهم وفطن لما بطن من أستنكارهم وحاذران

إن بعض الغن أثم   ثم قال يا رواة القنص وأشاه القول المربز أطاضة الجوهر

الشكو وقد ثل يا هامنتم من الزمان عبد الامتحان يكم أرجل أو ثان

7. In the city of Marrakesh, Morocco, children abandon their bicycles to listen to a story-teller

Parallel with the development of classical Arabic literature, a genre of popular story-telling has flourished throughout the Arabic-speaking wo
since pre-Islamic times. In the West its rich stock of narratives is best known through the translated anthologies of 'The Thousand and O
Nights'. The Hakawati, or story-teller, still frequents the bazaars and coffee houses of North Africa (7). His narratives of legendary her
provide a prized source of oral anecdote and popular imagery for contemporary theatre groups concerned to make their art responsive to the nee
and experiences of the ordinary people (8).

8. *A Jerusalem theatre group performs a 'Hakawati' in the occupied West Bank of Jordan*

9. *Mosul or Damascene Basin, 13th century AD. Inscribed for its recipient: '. . . the victorious, the director, the campaigner . . . the organiser, the possessor, al-Nāsir*

The use of the written word as a decorative art form became a speciality of Islamic art. As a symbol of identity, piety and sophistication calligraphic art is found on everything from buildings to coins. Even articles of a purely utilitarian character were elevated into 'objets d'art' by calligraphic embellishment. The crafts of metal-working and ceramics, though not of Islamic origin, were transformed by the artistic ingenuity of decoration in which the written word was incorporated into complex floral and geometrical designs. Less pleasing but equally indicative are the garish productions of contemporary tinsel art (10).

10. *Plaques decorated with verses from the Quran sold in the souks of Fez, Morocco*

11. *Iranian earthenware plaque. Late 12th early 13th century AD. Inscribed repeate with the word 'Happiny*

CHAPTER THREE

WAYS
OF
FAITH

A man with a book, a pool of shade and a circle of disciples. Sheikh Abd al-Raziq, sitting beneath an acacia and prodding the air with his much-thumbed manual of Islamic law, is the embodiment of orthodoxy. Around the old man his pupils crane forward – sitting in a circle, listening, asking questions.

This book is called *An Introduction to the Science of the Law*. It probes into everything and when it goes into something and finds that it is not in accordance with the Law it causes its destruction. Anything that is not contained in the Law must be discarded. If my mother or my father or my grandfather, Sheikh al-Obaid, or my teacher, Hassab al-Rasoul, told me something that was contrary to the Law, I would show them their error. I would say, 'No, it was this that the Law said.'

The scene is archetypal. It is how Islam has been expounded to the people for over 1300 years. This is how the Prophet first expounded God's law for mankind, and the faithful still discover anew something of its original drama in this superbly appropriate setting. As an image of religious instruction its fundamental immediacy must be the envy of every reformer, be he Christian, Hindu, or of whatever persuasion.

The scene is in fact in the Sudan, where Islam has been practised since the year 651. Sheikh Abd al-Raziq teaches at the mosque of Umduban, a village forty miles from Khartoum. For many Sudanese, Umduban is a place of great sanctity, a centre of prayer and pilgrimage. But what makes the scene of Abd al-Raziq's orthodox instruction all the more interesting is that the real focus of Umduban's celebrity is the tomb of Wad Badr, a Sufi brother who is revered as a saint.

The word 'sufi', meaning someone who wears only woollen homespun, was first applied to a group of Muslim ascetics in Kufa (Iraq) in the eighth century. It rapidly assumed a much wider connotation describing any Muslim individual or sect dedicated to a closer knowledge and love of God through worship, asceticism and initiation. To preserve the memory of a particularly devout practitioner disciples organised themselves into brotherhoods or orders and developed a variety of ritual and liturgical practices (including the chant or *dhikr*) designed to induce a heightened perception of the Divinity. These varied from respectable disciplines like fasting and meditation to the excesses of mass hysteria, intoxication and self-mutilation. Mystical experience was also seen as a mark of divine favour; the recipient became a vehicle for direct supernatural guidance in the form of spiritual leadership and a dispenser of *baraka*, the spiritual power that can work miracles.

Thus there are many elements in Sufism which are immediately recognisable to anyone familiar with popular Christianity – saint worship, monasticism, mysticism, miracles, liturgical chant, abstinence. The early popularity of Sufi practices coincided with the growth of mystic and gnostic practices in the Eastern Church, and the later evolution of large well-organised brotherhoods coincided with the establishment of the great monastic orders in the Roman church; there was undoubtedly much cross-fertilisation. But strands of Sufism can also be traced to other sources. Ascetic and meditational practices almost certainly owed something to Indian tradition. The chanting and dance of *dhikr* and a concern with exorcism were probably influenced by African ritual. And Sufi metaphysics expounding the different stages of initiation that lead to absorption in the Divinity appear to derive from neo-Platonism.

Such esoteric theories passed as high above the heads of the average devotee as did the scholarship of the *ulama*. In religion, as in literature, the illiterate masses had their own subculture, in this case itinerant preachers who spiced their Quranic exegesis not with dialectical subtleties but with lively narratives of heroism and piety. None too fastidious about the origins of their material they introduced a miscellany of legends drawn from Indian, Arabian and Christian tradition. Through them, many of the attributes and miracles ascribed to Jesus were transferred to Mohammed.

A hundred years ago it was estimated that in Egypt the entire population belonged to one or other of the Sufi brotherhoods. Sufism has since lost ground, especially in the cities, but millions of Muslims still follow its different brotherhoods. Umduban is only one of hundreds of such shrines from India to the Atlantic and, although by no means of world repute, it attracts pilgrims and pupils from as far as Nigeria, Cameroons and Chad. It is no exaggeration to say that on the African and Asian fringes of the Muslim world Islam and Sufism can be synonymous.

Wad Badr came to Umduban 150 years ago and founded there a Sufi brotherhood, dedicated to the belief that he had mystical powers to perform miracles that testified to a special religious favour in the eyes of God. His followers believe that this power of miraculous intervention is still exercised by his grandson, the present Khalifa (spiritual leader) of the brotherhood. The Khalifa and the brotherhood also manage the affairs of the shrine (including a highly rated Quranic school), well endowed with lands and new buildings financed by the donations of the faithful. Wad Badr belonged to the Qadiri order founded in Baghdad in the twelfth century by Abd al-Qadir al-Jilani, a member of the *ulama*, a jurist and philologist of distinction whose orthodoxy was unquestioned. A hint of mysticism in his approach to Revelation was not considered unsound, and if he was subsequently credited with miraculous powers he certainly never claimed any such thing during his lifetime. But at his shrine in Umduban we are in the realm of grace and miracles.

Any phenomenon that is not in accord with the Book and the Tradition cannot be called a miracle. It either belongs in the realm of black magic or it is mere charlatanism or – what shall I say? – an insult to the intelligence.

A pupil has asked Sheikh Abd al-Raziq about the goings-on at the tomb of Wad Badr. For when the devotees gather at the shrine the normally sober business of communal prayer is replaced by Sufi chanting and swaying to the music of drums, as mystics seek within themselves for an entranced experience of God. It is these rituals that challenge Sheikh Abd al-Raziq's austere and orthodox perception of Islam. At such times he must feel much like a Presbyterian before the grotto at Lourdes, a theologian amongst the Revivalists of the Bible Belt. Where is the scriptural justification for such 'excesses'? And how can the authority of the Book be maintained if one concedes the possibility of direct contact between the individual and God?

The origins of the Qadiri order illustrate the ambiguity of the relationship between the orthodox *ulama* and the Sufi brotherhoods – a relationship whose vicissitudes had as much to do with the fluid character of Sufi beliefs as with inconsistencies on the part of the *ulama*. A degree of tension still survives, as witnessed by the wary attitude of Sheikh Abd al-Raziq; and although it is now generally accepted that the Sufi emphasis on devotion can be justified from the Quran, it is significant that modern fundamentalist movements invariably begin with an outright rejection of what they see as Sufi concessions to idolatry, pantheism and obscurantism.

However, everyone concedes that since the thirteenth century the brotherhoods have been almost entirely responsible for Islam's missionary activity. In Africa they have taken the Word south and west of the Sahara so that in Senegal, for instance, the Muridiya brotherhood constitutes one of the most powerful economic groupings; thanks to a near monopoly of the peanut crop Senegalese saints drive around in Cadillacs. More typically, amongst the Berbers of Morocco and Algeria the brotherhoods have become closely associated with the underprivileged; here *baraka* was both an opiate and an outlet for the oppressed. In neighbouring Libya the Sanussi brotherhoods, who in the nineteenth century dominated the trade routes of the Sahara, acquired a formidable military reputation during a long and bloody struggle with colonialism.

With Islam, as with Christianity, the dogmas and precepts enshrined in Revelation, elaborated in Tradition and embodied in the Law do not entirely correspond with the beliefs and practices of many of those who call themselves Muslims. This is neither new nor surprising: even in an age of literacy the subtleties of theology are beyond the grasp of most and the practice of faith is more commonly a matter of habit or personal need than of systematic study. As one of the few still expanding religions, Islam owes its vitality as much to the popularity of shrines like that of Umduban as to the religious teaching of Sheikh Abd al-Raziq. There is nothing perverse, therefore, about including Sufism in a representative portrait of contemporary Islam. Indeed, from the toleration and the tension implicit in the relationship between the Sheikh and the Khalifa there is much to be learned about Islam's capacity for survival and renewal.

For all Muslims of whatever allegiance the Quran is, indisputably, the Word of God, perfect in every way, unassailable, more gospel by far than the Gospel.

When challenged by the sceptics of Mecca to prove that he was God's Messenger, the Prophet disdained performing a miracle. Instead he invited his critics to consider the Quran. Let them compose just ten verses comparable to those revealed to him by God. They declined; the task was impossible. In terms of truth, wisdom and language the Quran was demonstrably beyond the ingenuity of man. It was therefore acknowledged by the Prophet and the early Muslims as the one permissible miracle, the one example of direct divine intervention in the affairs of men.

It was also the total sum and the final instalment of Revelation, confirming and superseding the contributions of the prophets from Abraham onwards (including Moses and Jesus) but never itself to be superseded. It was the one miracle and only miracle, the Word and the last word. Unlike Christianity, Islam was not to have a Church. There was to be no hierarchy regulating the relationship between man and God and no Divine Regent clutching the keys of the gates of heaven and empowered with a guarantee of infallibility. The Word was the only authority.

Such precepts on matters of faith, conduct and ritual as are clearly laid down in the Quran are therefore accepted by all Muslims. By the brotherhood of Wad Badr as by Sheikh Abd al-Raziq the five universal precepts or 'pillars' of Islam are considered fundamental. At the school run by the brotherhood pupils are taught them as a sort of catechism.

'In the name of God, the Merciful, the Beneficent,' intones the teacher.

'In the name of God, the Merciful, the Beneficent,' repeat the five-year-olds.

'Islam is based on five principles.'
'Islam is based on five principles.'
First, 'The Testament.'
'The Testament.'
'That there is no god but God.'
'That there is no god but God.'
'And Mohammed is his Messenger . . .'
'And Mohammed is his Messenger . . .'

The testament, or *shahada,* of the One Supreme God is the first of the five pillars. It is not only an article of faith but, like the other four pillars, it constitutes an obligation. The Testament must be on every man's lips, proclaimed, recited, repeated. Faith without words has no place in Islam. The very word Islam, (and hence, from the same *s-l-m* root, Muslim) means 'submission' to the Almighty; and what is submission without evidence of it? The Quran is a guide to life and, more perhaps than any other religion, Islam takes its stand in the world of human affairs. The 'catechism' is therefore not a creed but a list of obligations.

Second, 'And observance of prayers.'
'And observance of prayers.'

Although the Quran does not specify the five daily prayers, they were already normal practice during the Prophet's lifetime and certainly the important midday prayers on Friday are specifically mentioned. So too is the muezzin, whose duty it is to call the faithful to prayer, and so too is the ritual of ablution before prayer. The prayers, consisting of set recitations from the Quran punctuated by kneeling, prostrations and bows, should preferably be performed communally and in unison. The physical routine in prayer echoes the prayer routine in daily life as measured by the inexorable muezzin. The week, the day and the hour, the body and the soul, are regulated by a pan-Islamic chronometer of religious observance. In Umduban, as everywhere else in the Islamic world, differences of opinion, of wealth, profession and race are all submerged for the performance of communal prayer. Orthodox Sheikh and Sufi brother stand side by side to pray together; neither demeans himself.

Third, 'And giving alms to the poor.'
'And giving alms to the poor.'

Again, this is an obligation intended primarily to provide tangible evidence of the individual's piety. But it also had a practical value; the community must care for its own, for its poor, its orphans, its travellers, if it was to realise the Quranic ideal of social unity. Almsgiving as an obligation is not quite the same as a tax – there was no procedure for enforcement – and even today the fiscal demands of the national state cannot be regarded as discharging the obligation. As proof one might cite the prosperity of Umduban, the new mosque, the flourishing school, the well-endowed brotherhood.

Fourth, 'And fasting at Ramadan.'
'And fasting at Ramadan.'

Ramadan is the ninth month of the lunar year. As the muezzin reminds the faithful that their days are divinely ordered, so Ramadan orders the year, leading it to a religious climax. Today, as ever, the Islamic world introverts itself for Ramadan. For a whole month the obligation to fast from dawn till dusk shatters the normal pattern of life. The tempo changes, traffic flags, shops close. It is a period of spiritual renewal and of the reaffirmation of Muslim ideals, the single most impressive display of Islamic solidarity.

Fifth, 'And the pilgrimage to the House,'
'And the pilgrimage to the House,'
'By those who have the means to undertake it.'
'By those who have the means to undertake it.'

The *haj,* the pilgrimage to Mecca, like almsgiving and Ramadan, has both evidential significance – as an indication of individual piety, and practical value – as a point of contact and intellectual exchange for the whole Islamic world. As Arabs and Persians, Indians and Africans, Sunnites and Shi'ites, jointly perform the great public ceremonials at Mecca they reaffirm the idea of Islamic unity. And as they succumb to the more reflective atmosphere of Medina, the burial place of the Prophet and the first home of the Islamic community, they renew their links with a past that epitomises that unity. As with Ramadan, there is a month for the *haj.* For those lacking 'the means to undertake it' – and how significant of the obligatory nature of the other pillars is that single exclusion clause – the month of pilgrimage is sometimes celebrated by a more modest journey. To shrines like that of Umduban the crowds are drawn and a sense of community is affirmed.

Had Islam remained the exclusive possession of the inhabitants of north-west Arabia it is possible that the Quran would have sufficed as a code of ritual and precept well suited to the local temperament and compensating for what it lacked in systematisation by its extraordinary inspirational power. For many sincere but unsophisticated believers from all over the Muslim world the five pillars are indeed sufficient; and by fundamentalists like the Wahabis of Saudi Arabia the purity of Quranic Revelation must be constantly re-emphasised as the only and exclusive source of authority.

But Islam was intended as a world religion regulating the affairs of men, not just Arabians, by universal acceptance of the Divine Law. As the Word spread with a rapidity that could only be proof of its destiny, so did the critical demands made upon it. What did this Quranic verse actually mean? How had the Prophet interpreted this precept or institutionalised that? What conclusions could be drawn from such and such a statement and how could it be reconciled with apparent contradiction elsewhere? Many felt the need to construct a comprehensive system of belief and law. Others, steeped in the traditions of the earlier religions, came to Islam with preconceived notions of what a religion should be, what questions it should answer and what needs fulfil. The religious law had to be elaborated, refined, standardised to accommodate these demands. Yet at the same time the original authority and purity of the Quran had to be preserved from dilution by over-much theological speculation.

The fact that Islam regulated the temporal as well as the spiritual sphere only complicated things further. The Prophet had named no successor and whereas this problem was largely solved by the acceptance of a Caliph as both secular and religious leader, the Caliph was not a Pope. He had no authority to define dogma or to authenticate Revelation. In constitutional terms he was the supreme head of the executive, not of the legislature. Who then was to shoulder this immense responsibility?

In the event the urgency of the task could not await the solution of this problem. The first compilation of the Quran was made at about the time of the Prophet's death and from a telling variety of sources – 'scraps of parchment and leather, tablets of stone, ribs of palm branches, camels' shoulder blades and spare ribs, pieces of board and the breasts of men'. Understandably, the earlier versions showed considerable variations. Othman, the third Caliph (644 – 56) ordered the scribes to produce a definitive version, and this became the standard text of the Quran.

By a more complex process, traditions (hadith) concerning the life and conduct of the Prophet were accumulated and sifted. Tradition, in the form of custom and precedent as established amongst the first Muslim community by the Prophet himself, was obviously a potent source of authority for the practical application of Quranic Law and doctrine and for their elaboration. For instance, whether or not it was implied in the Quran, if the Prophet had objected to divorce then clearly divorce was unacceptable, and so on. But given that for several generations such reports were handed down orally before being collected and committed to writing, they were obviously suspect. Consciously or unconsciously the pious might embroider them, the prejudiced slant them and schismatics invent them. And indeed this happened on a vast scale. Dynastic disputes among Muslims, and cultural confrontations between, for instance, Muslims and Christians, or Arabs and Persians can all be traced in the proliferating hadith of the early centuries.

Thus such a potentially solid and convenient source of legal and doctrinal legitimation was rendered almost useless. Or rather, it would have been had it not been for the monumental weight of painstaking scholarship that was simultaneously brought to bear on the subject. The authentication of hadith became a major discipline and one of consummate importance since not only did points of ritual and of faith depend on it but also the foundations of Islamic law as both a science and a code of practice. Moreover, this discipline was one that greatly influenced the development of Arabic scholarship. For the method of authentication was essentially scientific and analytic, a meticulous investigation of each hadith leading to its classification and eventual acceptance or rejection.

To establish its provenance each hadith was prefaced with a list of the names of those who had passed it on. These genealogies inevitably began with one of the Prophet's companions and ended with whoever had first recorded the hadith in writing. The list could be long, and the scrutiny and validation of names spawned a separate discipline concerned exclusively with biographical compilations. Armed, courtesy of the biographers, with a *Who's Who* of the Islamic world in the seventh and eighth centuries, the hadith scholar set to work evaluating the moral character, retentive powers and general honesty of each authority. Account was also taken of whether the hadith itself was consistent with Quranic Revelation and with other hadith. Given that there were at least 200,000 such reports in circulation the task was enormous and the system of classification reflected its complexity. But basically there were 'sound', 'good' and 'weak' categories and, as the wheat was slowly sifted from the chaff, the task assumed more manageable proportions. In the mid-ninth century the first critical compilations of hadith appeared. These, the *Sahih* of Al-Bukhari and Muslim, acquired an almost definitive status and although they by no means exhausted hadith scholarship they enshrined the main body of authenticated tradition which, along with the Quran, was now acknowledged as the source of all authority in matters of Islamic doctrine and law.

Of course hadith scholars, like hadith narrators, were not without their quota of human frailty and therefore potentially just as liable to err and distort. But in hadith scholarship, as in Quranic and legal scholarship, this danger was theoretically eliminated by invoking the important principle of *ijma* or consensus. This notion of consensus became the equivalent, in an egalitarian society, of the divine right of kings or the infallibility of the papacy.

Islam countenanced no clergy; all men were equal before God and no power must intervene between man and God. Great emphasis is also placed on the importance of communal awareness and communal worship. The first Muslim community founded and led by the Prophet in Medina was taken as a model of Muslim society and revered as so perfect that it must have been directly guided by God. This guidance was identified as being expressed through the consensus of the community and subsequently remained immanent in the community. Thus, after the death of the Prophet, one of its first manifestations was in the consensus of acceptance which created the Caliphate. *Ijma*, according to Professor Gibb, underwrote the whole system of Islamic doctrine and alone gave it its final validity.

For it is *ijma* in the first place which guarantees the authenticity of the text of the Quran and of the Traditions. It is *ijma* that determines how the words of their texts are to be pronounced and what they mean and in what direction they are to be applied. But *ijma* goes much further; it is erected into a theory of infallibility, a third channel of revelation. The spiritual prerogative of the Prophet – the Muslim writers speak of them as the 'light of Prophecy' – were inherited (in the Sunni doctrine) not by his successors in the temporal government of the community, the Caliphs, but by the community as a whole.

But how was the consensus of a community which soon embraced half the known world to be determined? The answer, of course, was that only the consensus of those directly concerned with theological and legal matters was relevant – in other words, the intelligentsia or, in Islamic terms, the *ulama*, the 'learned'.

Some Muslims did not, however, accept the idea of *ijma*. The Shi'ites (i.e. 'partisans') claimed that Ali, the Prophet's son-in-law and his successors were the only legitimate Caliphs (or in Shi'i parlance, 'Imams'). Their dynastic protest also masked a regional and social protest against the Umayyad aristocracy and their patronage of Damascus. But the movement rapidly attracted other disaffected elements and acquired a strong doctrinal base which, amongst other things, reserved for the Imams the authority in matters of hadith validation and jurisprudence which followers of the Sunna (i.e. tradition, custom) attributed to the consensus (*ijima*) of the religious experts (*ulama*).

In the first two centuries of Islam, pending the emergence of a consensus, the scholar was free to exercise his own reason and judgement on legal matters. The door was thus ajar to creative innovation and logical rationalisation. But as each problem of authenticity or interpretation was resolved, the stamp of *ijma* meant that that particular matter was basically settled. Although the Quran only specifically dealt with a fraction of all human activities, the scope of these pronouncements clearly showed that the religious law was to take cognisance of all, from the bathroom to the battlefield, from the cradle to the grave. By a process analogous to that of hadith scholarship, all cognisable activities were classified – they were either 'obligatory', 'desirable', 'permissible', 'objectionable' or 'prohibited' – and were eventually enshrined in legal equivalents of the doctrinal *al-Sahih*. These were the foundations of the celebrated *madhahib* – 'ways' or schools – of Islamic Law (known after their founders as the Hanafi, Maliki, Shafi'i and Hanbali) which emerged in the late eighth and ninth centuries. They were not sects; only in the finest points of detail did they differ from one another and each was, and is, equally acceptable. Nor, in practice, were they definitive codes. Legal judgments took account of local custom in different parts of the Islamic world and of the interests of the secular power. Nevertheless, the *sharia*, meaning the 'highway' or 'the straight and narrow' of the law, enjoyed the same aura of permanence and immutability as theological dogma.

To assume, however, that such rigidity necessarily implied sterility or paralysis would be wrong. For one thing it was always regarded as a positive and wondrous asset. Without a pole star of true and constant Revelation ordering the religious and secular life of the community the Islamic firmament could hardly have held together. For another, the *ulama* who guarded and expounded the religious law proved a remarkably responsible and responsive body. Their role in different parts of the world and at different stages in time varied enormously but always it was highly influential. Indeed, without at least the tacit support of the *ulama* the secular power could scarcely govern. Or put another way, because of the authority of the *ulama*, the Arab-Islamic world was able to survive and even flourish long after empire had passed from its hands into those of Mongols, Turks and Europeans. In short, the system worked. In an impermanent world the *ulama*, armed with an authority based on divine Revelation (and thus able to monopolise education and administration as well as the law and religion) gave to society a resilience and stability that have rarely been equalled.

And finally, rigidity did not mean intolerance. Contrary to received ideas, Islam has generally proved unusually indulgent towards religious dissent, a point amply illustrated by the proliferation of beliefs and practices which are generally lumped together under the name of Sufism.

* * *

Outside the shrine of Wad Badr in Umduban, the women gossip away the anxious moments of waiting. One has a daughter who is sick. Another has come because she always does; she has been coming for twenty years. It is a matter of loyalty. The Khalifa is her patron.

'He is the sheikh of our faith and I believe in him. Once my husband had someone released on bail. The man jumped bail and the court sentenced my husband to prison. We had seven children.'
'How terrible.'
'The youngest, a son, was fourteen'.
'How dreadful for you.'
'I came with my family to the Khalifa to tell him about our misfortune and about what had happened to the children's father; also that we had no one else to look after us. The Khalifa recited the first verse |of the Quran| and told me that, God willing, my husband would soon be released. And at twelve o'clock on the very day of my return from the Khalifa, I came home to find the father of my children waiting for me there.'
'How wonderful and may God grant him health and long life. But, you know, what he has done for you is only a small thing. His powers are much greater.'
'The Khalifa is miraculous, miraculous.'
'Yes, he performs great miracles, great miracles, great miracles.'

The women have faith. They accept the Quran, they obey the law and they perform the five pillars. But they believe in the Khalifa. Although they would be the first to agree that his powers must be from God, they would not welcome the news that Quranic tradition specifically excludes any such mediator between man and God. Neither would they credit the suggestion that saint worship, like that accorded to Wad Badr, is also proscribed and that the only miracle in Islam is the Quran itself.

The point is simply that Sufism represents not just the heterodoxy of Islam but its eclecticism. It is not a system of beliefs and practices to rival those of the religious law, but a reaction made possible by the existence and acceptance of the religious law. 'A series of different and even contradictory experiments' is the definition of Sufism ventured by one scholar (Clifford Geertz) and supported by a wealth of recent anthropological studies of the different Sufi orders; 'less a definite standpoint in Islam, a distinct conception of religiousness like Methodism ... than a diffuse expression of that necessity ... for a world religion to come to terms with the variety of mentalities, the multiplicity of local forms of faith, and yet maintain the essence of its own identity.'

Sheikh Abd al-Raziq agrees. He may not approve of the brotherhood's way, but in answer to a question from one of his pupils, he concedes that it has some value.

'The Sufis invented these practices in order to attract a more plebeian audience. When such people had gathered around them and become followers they taught them the more serious aspects of religion and then let them go.' Of course, none of his own pupils would come into this category. 'Yes, these practices were invented to attract the mob.'

'But this way they wouldn't have just been a mob.' For one pupil the *dhikr* is more than just window dressing. 'They would have gathered for a certain purpose: to be instructed.'

'No, but I told you it was only a means to an end.'

'A means?'

'Yes, a means. Not an end in itself.'

The obligation of prayer is one of the five 'pillars' of Islam enjoined in the Quran. Ideally it should be performed in a mosque, but since the hours of prayer, the wording, the movements and the orientation of the worshipper are all laid down, the act of prayer performed anywhere is an assertion of identity with the whole Muslim community.

Pilgrims praying at Mecca in Saudi Arabia

2. 'Vue de la Mecque', by D'Ohssen, 19th century

Another obligation incumbent on all Muslims of sufficient means is that of the 'haj', or pilgrimage to Mecca and Medina. In all the cities of Islamic world the departure of the 'haj' caravan and its eventual return (3) were highlights of the year. Even today returning pilgrims record the incidents of the journey in paintings on the walls of their houses (4).

3. (above right) 'View of the Grand Procession of the Sacred Camel through the Streets of Cairo on their Pilgrimage to Mecca and Medina', by Cooper Williams. 19th ce

4. (below right) Gaziret Quoma, Egypt. His 'haj' painting shows that the pilgrim has travelled by boat and aeroplane to arrive at the 'Kaaba' (bottom, left hand co

5. The Great Mosque
of al-Hakam II in
Cordoba, Spain. 10th
century

6. The Mosque of Ahmed Ibn Tulun,
Cairo, 876-879

7. The Great Mosque of al-Mutawakkil at
Samarra in Iraq (848-52). In this case the
minaret is ascended via a spiral track instead
of stairs because, it is said, the Mosque's first
muezzin preferred to ride up on his donkey.

The mosque originated as a site on which the whole Islamic community could assemble for prayer and instruction. Its prototype was the wall
enclosure of the Prophet's home in Medina. Gradually certain requirements of worship assumed architectural forms. A shaded area for the
faithful, originally supplied by a covering stretched between standing palm trunks, was translated into stone or brick pillars with a dome or vau
This basic hypostyle unit had the advantage of being capable of repetitious extension as the community grew (5).

The 'Mihrab', signifying the place of the Prophet, was shown as an arched and empty recess in the 'qibla' wall (8); the need for ablutio
resulted in elaborate pools and fountains often shaded with a dome (6, 8), and the needs of the muezzin led to the construction of minarets (7
With other additions, including cloistered walls and gates, an integral architectural unit emerged.

9. *Sheikh Abd al-Razik in the mosque at Umduban*

10. *Children from the Quranic school perform their abulutions before prayer*

11. *Members of the Sufi order chant the 'dhikr'*

At Umduban in the Sudan the practice of faith centres on the well endowed shrine of Wad Badr with its new mosque. Wad Badr was a Sufi sai *through whose grace (invoked by the drums and chant of* dhikr *(11)) worshippers aspire to a personal experience of God. Yet at the same shrin* *the orthodox Sheikh Abd al-Razik (9) propounds the sacred law; and the five 'pillars' or Quranic Revelation, including prayer and ablutio* *(10), are zealously observed.*

12. *Sunset prayer outside the tomb of Wad Badr in Umduban*

13. *The minaret of the mosque and the dome of the tomb of Wad Badr peak over the trees at Umduban*

CHAPTER FOUR

THE MUSLIM CITY

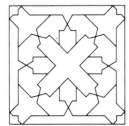

To describe Islamic society as traditionally urban has become something of a cliché. The history of the Middle East is the history of its cities, where commerce and learning, industry and art, government and faith flourished. With a few rare but notable exceptions the hinterland boasted no provincial chateaux, no stately homes or country houses; the Arab world has never known a landed gentry with rural power bases – no feudal barons to hold the king to ransom and no squirearchy to demand, and then manipulate, the franchise. Power bases were, and still largely are, urban. Military chiefs often formed armies from men of the desert or mountain, and led them to conquer the cities. But once they established their power, their interests lay in a stable and prosperous urban life. Baghdad, Damascus, Cairo and Fez testify to the continued political and social dominance of city over countryside

Many of these cities – Baghdad, Cairo, Qayrawan – were actually founded by the Arabs; the others were enlarged and enriched by them. How was it that an eruption of bedouin tribes from the deserts of Arabia produced an empire of glittering cities? Six hundred years later a similar eruption, this time of Mongols from Central Asia, would have exactly the opposite effect; towns and cities were obliterated, civilisation ravaged. But the Arabs destroyed practically nothing. Following the Prophet's death in AD 632 they took just over a century to amass one of the greatest empires in history. They did so almost entirely by force of arms yet at practically no cost to civilisation. Instead of demolishing the Roman, Byzantine and Sassanian heritage, they conceived the idea of upstaging it. Sixty years after the Prophet's death they signified their arrival on the world scene by building the Dome of the Rock on one of the most hallowed sites in Jerusalem, a city then widely portrayed as situated at the dead centre of the world. Twenty years later came the great Umayyad mosque in Damascus, today still one of the noblest buildings in the Islamic world and then surely nothing short of a wonder. And fifty years on, in AD 762, Baghdad was under construction, the first integrally planned Arab capital.

Meanwhile in North Africa the site of the Qayrawan had been chosen and a start made on what was to develop into the most classical of Arab mosques. To the east, Fustat, the main Arab settlement in Egypt since 640, grew into a major city and was enlarged in 969

70

by the Fatimid foundation of Al-Qahira, Cairo. And in the west, following the conquest of Spain in the eighth century, a princely refugee from the power struggles in Baghdad, Idris Ibn Abdallah, lit upon a well-watered valley that nestled in the skirts of the Atlas and abreast the road to Spain. There in 788-9 was founded the city of Fez.

Seen from the low hills above, the densely packed houses of Fez follow the valley's contours in gentle terraces, their flat roofs a quartzy jumble of dazzling cubes. It looks like a mosaic without pattern, a city spawned without logic. And yet there is both pattern and logic; and what is more significant, it is a logic that was shared by the other great Muslim cities before the dawn, in the nineteenth century, of a new universal culture whose sources are in the West.

Like all its Arab counterparts the Fez of today is formed of an aggregation of cities. Its nuclei are the Andalusian city settled by craftsmen from Cordoba and the Qarawiyin city settled by merchants from Qayrawan. The former settled on the south bank of the Wadi Fez, the latter on the north bank. In 1070 Yusuf Ibn Tashfin of the Almoravid dynasty founded a further city upstream; at the same time he demolished the walls between the two original cities and bridged the river. Two hundred years later Sultan Abu Yusuf (1258-86) of the Merinid dynasty, the Medicis of Fez, built Fez Jdid, or New Fez, a royal and administrative capital, still further upstream. Fez was growing less by natural expansion than by royal patronage. 'A world it is to see how large, how populous, how well-fortified and walled this citie is,' wrote Leo Africanus in his *Description of Africa* in 1526. The man who became known in Europe as Leo from Africa – Leo Africanus – was properly Hasan al-Wazzan, born in Granada but brought up in Fez. In fact in Africa he was usually known as Al-Fasi, the man from Fez, and his chronicles are testimony to his attachment to the sixteenth-century city.

Today 'New Fez' is not the compact Merinid foundation but yet another creation. When in 1911, after years of interference and exploitation, French troops finally moved into Morocco, they found Fez much as it had been in Leo Africanus's day. They viewed Fez as a uniquely preserved and uniquely beautiful relic of the Middle Ages. General Lyautey imposed the equivalent of a preservation order and laid out a new city, three miles to the west, that then became the colonial and industrial centre of modern Fez. The old city – or cities – remains, somewhat down-at-heel, its population swollen by immigrants from the countryside, its elite dispersed to the new city, to Rabat, Casablanca and overseas.

Like many of the great houses of old Fez, the Tazi family palace is 'closed' now; its courtyard of mosaic tiles is sprouting weeds, its fountains have been drained. The last

Pasha of Fez lived here. He and his brothers in the finance and commerce ministries were the descendants of a long line of urban bourgeois elites, strategically placing themselves – here as health inspector, there as palace treasurer – until the whole pulse of the Muslim city flowed through them. The great grand-nephews of the Pasha are still situating themselves with acumen: one is Secretary of State in the Foreign Office; another is a senior official in the Labour Ministry; another an official in the Royal Armed Forces; but their houses are no longer in Fez and the universal culture of their day finds apter expression in the city of New York than in any city of the Arab world.

It was in 1953 that the young Abdelmalek Tazi persuaded his father, a grand-nephew of the Pasha, to move out of the old city, the *medina*, of Fez into the 'nouvelle' French city. This youngest of four sons had already created a precedent: seeing how well he excelled in Quranic school, his father concocted a dream that *this* son should become a religious scholar. He himself was a health inspector in the city, safeguarding the public health against the sale of rotten or exposed foods, overseeing the cleaning of streets and sewage disposal. But he was well-acquainted with religious scholars at the Great Mosque of Fez, the Qarawiyin, and he often went there in the course of a day to listen to their instruction. By the age of five Abdelmalek had already studied at Quranic school for three years; he was then moved to a private traditional Arabic school where he studied the Arabic language and culture exclusively for four more years. It was now that his father thought of sending him to the *madrassah* of the Qarawiyin, that his older brothers intervened. At nine Abdelmalek was sent out of the *medina* to a lycée in the 'nouvelle ville' and by the time he was fourteen he had persuaded his father to live outside the old city as well. Later Abdelmalek was to live in Europe for eleven years and take a German wife, but it was at the point of his departure from the *medina* of Fez that he left the culture of a civilisation that was once almost universal and entered that of another.

Al-Madinah means simply the city. *Din* is an Aramaic word meaning judgment or decision in the legal sense and al-Madinah is the place where judgements are made. Every Arab city is therefore al-Madinah. But al-Madinah is also of course one specific city. When, after the Prophet's death, the Arab armies began to fan out across the Middle East and North Africa, they brought with them their language, their faith and, as part of that faith, the vision of a new society. The vision was not a dream, but a proven reality. For the new society was already alive and flourishing; it was to be found in a remote city on the Red Sea caravan route, al-Madina.

Non-Arabs know it simply as Medina, a centre of Islamic pilgrimage second in importance only to its near neighbour, Mecca. In Mecca the Prophet was born; there the word was first revealed to him and there, on the ancient site of Abraham's sacrifice, Islam staked its claim to be the legitimate successor, and superseder of the Judaic-Christian tradition. But it was in Medina that the Prophet founded the first Islamic community. The year 622, the date of the *hijra*, when the Prophet decided to flee Mecca for the safety of the *din* – of the city he renamed Medina – marks the beginning of the Islamic calendar and the beginning of the Islamic state. Medina remained the capital under the first three Caliphs and came to be regarded as the norm of community life and the prototype, in many ways the ideal, of the Islamic city.

For Christians the ideal of the just and ordered city has usually provided an analogy for Paradise. St Augustine's City of God did boast a few citizens here on earth. They were the good and the loving, but they were exiles in the earthly city until all men were of like mind or until Paradise beckoned. Likewise the heavenly city of Renaissance art. Christ the King on his throne flanked by Seraphim and Cherubim, saints, doctors of religion and martyrs could be a comforting idea; it might be hierarchical, but the densely packed foreground suggested standing room for all. The ideal was worth aspiring to. By contrast the Islamic City was for the here and now. The ideal represented by Medina, in which the citizenry were united in obedience to the Prophet in matters both spiritual and temporal, was not only worth pursuing but obligatory. The Law regulated, in some detail, both social behaviour and religious practice. By implication the two formed a continuum and, although on the day of Judgment each man would stand alone, he would be judged on his performance in society. Without detracting from the individual's responsibility to seek salvation the Quran and the statements of the Prophet (the Hadith) repeatedly emphasised the importance of the community. The community must worship together; by almsgiving and charitable endowments it must provide for all its members. A consensus of the community was a guarantee against it straying into error, and mutual exhortation was essential for the generation of good works and the propagation of the faith.

To the Prophet the idea of men retreating into isolation to better their chances in the hereafter was anathema. 'No monkery in Islam' he declared in unequivocal terms. Celibacy and other forms of worldly renunciation were equally self-seeking and suspect. Islam was not merely a new religion but a new social order, a new kind of state. It is impossible to overemphasise the point. Where salvation lies with the community as a whole, the community is worth fighting for. Islam throve on victory, striking city after city and superimposing the new order on the pinnacles of whatever authority preceded it. And where there was no social edifice of substance the Islamic armies laid out their camps, summoned settlers, and set about building a city. The new cities, whether integrally planned like Baghdad or aggregated like Cairo and Fez, were an opportunity to give concrete expression to the ideals of the Islamic state.

The first impression of Fez is that the city was clearly not built for effect. Vistas, boulevards, waterfronts and façades are conspicuous by their absence. Leo Africanus thought the fortified walls worthy of remark. But walls contain those within as well as discourage those without; and after the walls, the thing which impressed him most was the crowds. The city was not a collection of magnificent buildings but a congregation of people. Whether rich or poor, their homes were not detached in gardens, not even semi-detached in terraces, but huddled hard together, three walls shared and the fourth blankly shutting off the street. 'Believer is to believer,' said the Prophet, 'as the mutually upholding sections of a building.' As each member of the community is a dependent part of the whole so each house is part of its neighbours. The city is one vast condominium.

At street level the mud walls are continuous and blank save for heavy doors. Each door opens into a twisted narrow passage at the end of which, hidden from view of the street, a very different image of Islam is revealed. For the centre of the house is a courtyard, flanked on three sides by galleries, with a fountain or a pool in the middle. The courtyard will be paved and perhaps dotted with parterres, the walls and the pillars supporting the galleries may have faience tiling and carved or stucco capitals. It is a place of unexpected elegance and charm, a sanctuary for the family, as hallowed and precious as the city is to the community. Traditionally, the father is the *imam* who leads his family in prayer just as the *imam* of the mosque leads the whole community. Each house though set within the structural pattern of the city, is closed to the city and open to the sky. It thus affirms the individual's direct relationship with God whilst still within the context of society.

The open patios of the houses find their communal equivalent in the open space at the centre of the city. This is the mosque. Fez has dozens of mosques but here as in every other Arab city, a distinction is made between the Jami mosque and the local mosques. 'City mosques are of two kinds,' wrote Ibn Khaldun the fourteenth-century historian and statesman-*manqué* who spent much of his early career at Fez; 'great spacious ones which are prepared for holiday prayers, and other minor ones which are restricted to one section of the population or one quarter of the city and which are not for the generally attended prayers.' The Masjid Jami, the 'great spacious one', was the centre of worship for the whole city. It had to be large enough to enable everyone to assemble there. In Medina the courtyard of the Prophet's house served this purpose and thus became the first mosque and the prototype for all later developments. It seems to have been simply a

74

large walled area, perhaps fifty metres square, with a shaded section at each end formed by thatch supported on rows of palm trunks. One of these areas was on the south side and served to indicate the *qibla*, the correct orientation to ensure that the faithful prayed facing Mecca.

The basic requirements of the early mosque were therefore a large open but defined space with a shaded area at the appropriate end. To these were soon added other details and architectural forms so that well before the time Fez was founded the mosque had progressed from a courtyard to a building. To call the faithful to prayer, the early muezzin stood on a roof top. But church towers suggested a better idea and for a new religion trying to upstage its established rivals an essential one; hence the minaret.

In Fez each of the twin cities of earliest times, Andalusian and Qarawiyin, boasted a Masjid Jami. Each dates from the middle of the ninth century but it was the Qarawiyin mosque (the mosque which, centuries later, Abdelmalek's father liked to frequent) that was subsequently favoured by royal patronage. According to the quaint seventeenth-century English of Leo Africanus's translator, it was 'of so incredible a bigness that the circuit thereof and of the buildings belonging unto it is a good mile and a half about'. Seen from the air the Qarawiyin mosque – and to a lesser extent the Andalusian mosque – appears as a spacious ordered clearing at the heart of the *medina*'s architectural jungle. As a gathering point at the community's focal centre, it fills the same role as a Roman forum or European market square, but with one important difference; in the Islamic city the sanction under which the community foregathers is not that of political or corporate authority but of religious hegemony. The call to prayer resounds from the minaret five times a day; it is the pulse of the city. For noon prayers on Friday the whole population courses down the twisted arteries of the *medina* to converge on the Jami Masjid. In the city's circulatory system the mosque is truly the heart, animating the whole urban being and affirming its unity and interdependence.

Just as Islam regulated much more than the religious affairs of the community, so the mosque was much more than a place of worship. The Qarawiyin mosque remained until this century the foremost educational institution in Fez. Like Al Azhar in Cairo it was the city's college. Here the elite of pupils who had emerged from the local Quranic schools and had then passed through the hands of semi-official crammers, embarked on their higher education (as Tazi wished his son to do). Within the precincts of the mosque they sat in circles round their chosen professor and entered the great realms of Islamic learning. Scholarship was not only held in high regard but automatically conferred authority and consequence. As the student absorbed his professor's commentaries on the

Quran and Hadith, as he explored the sciences and arts, and above all as he joined the debate on matters of Islamic jurisprudence, so he approached the status of the *ulama*, the learned and immensely influential caucus of Muslim society.

Since all knowledge is of God, support of the *ulama* and deference to them were obligatory. And since all man's actions come under divine law, the *ulama* as the elite entrusted with its interpretation were in a position of great influence. To them were referred all the details of daily life which required legal sanction, including business contracts, marriages and endowments. And it was from the ranks of the *ulama* that state administrators were drawn. Such posts admittedly were few and the procedures of consultation were informal and irregular; but whether in official, legal, academic or religious employ members of the *ulama* constituted both the nervous system and the conscience of the city.

In Fez, as in other cities, the actual seat of government was somewhat apart from the *medina* proper. The royal household and palace, the barracks, treasury and civil service were located in Fez Jdid, the 'new' city built by the Merinids. But this should not be seen to imply the real separation of secular and religious authority.

It did, however, imply that the 'old' city was in a sense self-sufficient. In the early days of Islam the Prophet and his immediate successors in the Caliphate had exercised both spiritual and temporal authority over the community. The Caliph led the Friday prayers in the mosque, interpreted the law, headed the government and directed the armed forces. But with the spread of Islam, disputes over the Caliphate, the emergence of satellite dynasties, and the inevitable difficulties of uniting so many responsibilities in one person, this unitary leadership was gradually diluted. Through regents, ministers and governors the ruler still exercised political and fiscal authority and he remained the supreme religious leader. But his judicial role was delegated to the *qadi* and the *qadi* in turn appointed the *imam*, or prayer leader, of each mosque. Both *imam* and *qadi* were members of the *ulama* and their appointment had to be acceptable to the *ulama*. In no sense could the city prosper without a strong leader and without the protection, authority and legitimacy that was implied. But it could, and during the confused power struggles of the Middle Ages, it did survive frequent intrigues in the royal palace, and traumatic upheavals on the battlefield. Had the palace of Fez Jdid stood side by side with the Qarawiyin mosque, the stability of the *medina* would have been in question. As it was, through five hundred years of political eclipse when Turks, Portuguese, Spanish and French intrigued with its rulers, Fez remained an oasis of Arab Islamic government and learning.

Around the Qarawiyin mosque are located most of the *madrassahs*. Except for the famous and favoured Abu Inan *madrassah* at the western end of the city, the Fez *madrassahs* were more student hostels than teaching establishments. They had halls of prayer, some even had a minaret, but they were essentially the academic equivalents of the inns for visiting merchants which were also located near the mosque. Of these latter establishments Leo Africanus reckoned there were 'almost two hundred', and to them came a continuous stream of merchants, encouraged by the city's location at the crossroads of two vital trade routes: the long east-west route from Tunis (Ifriqiya) and Egypt to Spain and the Atlantic coast, and the no less gruelling trans-Saharan route from the kingdoms of Timbuktu and the Upper Niger to the Mediterranean. They brought to Fez the luxuries of the whole Muslim world – gems and sandalwood from India, furs from Central Asia, incense from Yemen, pearls from the Gulf, saffron, indigo and carpets from Iran, gold and slaves from West Africa. And they took away the products of Fez, the silks, thread, and fabrics, the saddlery and the shoes.

The area beside the Qarawiyin mosque is the *qisariya*, the commercial centre of the whole city. Here in the narrow streets and cul-de-sacs are jewellers' shops, a whole bazaar for shoes and leather goods, another for spices and another for fabrics. Here too are the *funduqs*, the warehouses of each trade where goods are sold by auction from wholesaler to retailer. Local markets elsewhere in the city deal in foodstuffs and basic commodities but the *qisariya* is the prestigious luxury emporium. Its proximity to the mosque marks it as such; for, far from condemning trade, Islam smiles on it. The two essentials for drawing closer to God are piety and usefulness to the community. Usefulness means not just good behaviour and worthy endeavour but actively promoting the community's welfare by enriching it and endowing it. A profitable investment made in the course of a visit to the mosque is, according to the Quran, 'a bounty from your Lord'. Indeed the *ulama* themselves often made their living by engaging in crafts and trade.

The official who presided over the market was himself from the *ulama*. This was the *muhtasib*, a man of great importance in Fez where the institution lingered on long after it had been superseded in other parts of the Arab world. The *muhtasib* was the guardian of public morality and as such his responsibilities were legion and diverse. He saw to it that the Fast and the Friday prayers were observed and he also kept an eye on decent public conduct in, for instance, the baths and inns. The humane treatment of children, slaves and animals was his concern, as was the cleanliness of the streets and mosques. But his principal function was as supervisor and arbitrator in matters commercial. He checked on weights and measures – his standard cubit is still to be seen marked on a marble slab in the *qisariya*; he set prices, exercised a system of quality control, punished fraud and settled industrial disputes. To assist him he had representatives drawn from each of the separate trades and crafts; like other officials he was obliged to consult informed opinion. But however mundane his duties it is significant that the post of *muhtasib* was considered to be a religious institution. The incumbent was practising at a collective level that obligation of the individual to exhort his fellows to good and to denounce evil. He was the *sharia* in action, a classical example of how Islam entered daily life and inspired the Muslim community with a sense of solidarity and conformity.

The *muhtasib* also oversaw the distribution of water, an important function in all Arab cities and nowhere more so than in Fez. Doubtless it was the vision of clear springs welling from the ground and rushing to form the Wadi Fez that dictated the site of the city. It was certainly to the river – to the convenience and abundance of clear mountain water – that the city owed its subsequent development and prosperity. The flow of the Wadi Fez, little affected by seasonal variations, has been estimated as providing the Fasi people with exactly double the per capita consumption of New Yorkers. Using the natural fall of the land, and conducting supplies by an elaborate system of channels and conduits, the engineers of Fez brought water to every mosque, *madrassah* and *funduq*, to the street fountains and the public baths, and to every household of consequence. There was even enough supply and sufficient fall to operate an effective system of flushing drains.

In all this, public health and cleanliness were priorities duly enjoined by religious law. In addition water was needed for purely ritual purposes. 'When ye rise up to prayer,' says the Quran, 'wash your face and your hands to the elbows and wipe your heads and your feet to the ankles.' Thus every mosque had a pool or faucets and when prayers are said in private, as in the domestic courtyard, there too should be water.

But what made the water the lifeblood of the city was the opportunities it offered for agriculture and industry. The proximity of good grazing and arable land was an obvious necessity for any medieval city. In Fez extensive fruit and vegetable gardens were able to flourish both within and without the city limits. Beyond, the mountain pastures supplied meat, the olive groves oil, and the coastal plain grain. The essentials for growth were there. But to create the wealth to realise it, Fez turned to industry.

In both English and French, Morocco denotes leather and Fez denotes a hat. Both the city and the country of which it is the ancient capital became known by their products. Ever since craftsmen from Andalusia settled on the south bank of the river, Fez has been famous for its handicrafts. During the prolonged death throes of Arab rule in Spain there were further influxes of refugees from Cordoba, Seville and Granada. An artistic and industrious people, they brought with them skills, music and learning unheard of before. They endowed the city with its gracious mosques, stuccos and mosaics and they filled the streets with the clamour of their trades.

Some trades, like the working of precious metals (a speciality of the important Jewish community), weaving and leather finishing required little or no water and could therefore be conducted in the heart of the city. But others, pottery and milling and, above all, dyeing and tanning, required vast quantities. Hence they were located downstream of the residential and commercial areas and added another considerable dimension to the city plan.

'Dyers have their abode by the river's side and have each of them a most clear fountain or cistern to wash their silk-stuffs in,' noted Leo Africanus. This was in the 1520s; the dyers are still there today. So are the tanneries, now four in number, where skins and hides are scraped, stretched and then cured in a variety of evil-smelling vats. Twenty different operations are involved in the processing alone – a good reason for production-line methods. But the tanneries are not factories so much as communal workshops to which the craftsman brings his own team of apprentices and journeymen, his own tools and materials, and in which he rents space and facilities. There may be a hundred such teams in one tannery.

How, in the traditional Islamic city, all this labour was organised is the subject of a surprisingly acrimonious debate. Were the trade organisations to which, for instance, each tannery belonged, 'guilds' or not? They certainly never achieved the corporate independence or aspired to the political clout of their European equivalents. But in Fez at any rate they were important institutions. Headed by an *amin*, they regulated the internal hierarchy of each trade, operated a system of initiation, settled internal disputes, and provided the *muhtasib* with a consensus of opinion within each trade and with specialised advice on trade practices. They also operated a rudimentary system of social benefits for their members, held annual parades and organised hunting vacations. Each 'guild' patronised certain mosques (in addition, of course, to attending the Masjid Jami) and identified with certain Sufi brotherhoods.

* * *

Umma, the Arabic word for 'community', makes no distinction between the citizen body of each city and the world-wide Muslim community. The laws and institutions which bound each citizen of Fez to his urban community were common to every Arab city; the degree of uniformity was such – in language, law, custom and scholarship – that one can truly speak of a universal society.

Attendance at the Friday prayers in the Masjid Jami was the most dramatic manifestation of communal solidarity within the city. Its equivalent for the universal society of Islam was the *haj*, the pilgrimage to Mecca and Medina. Undoubtedly this was the single greatest incentive to travel within the Islamic world. And just as a visit to the mosque might be combined with a business deal, so the *haj* became an opportunity for commercial exchange and professional advancement. The vast annual *haj* caravan that set off from Fez was laden with merchandise; a fairly impoverished pilgrim like Leo Africanus expected to work his passage, either by providing secretarial services or by speculation on merchandise.

The accounts of medieval travellers and scholars – and of their many less well-known contemporaries – give a vivid picture of the Muslim city in the late Middle Ages. All of them were highly educated members of the *ulama* and what immediately strikes the reader is the ease and confidence with which they could move within the elite, from Cordoba to Fez, from Fez to Cairo, from Cairo to Damascus and so on. Wherever they went they could expect respect, hospitality and employment: at any one time at least half the *ulama* in the city of Damascus came from outside its bounds.

The historian Ibn Khaldun, for instance, was born in Tunis in 1332, but spent several interrupted years in Merinid employ at Fez, first as the writer of the *alama* (the ruler's official signature), later as an official member of the Sultan Abu Ishak's literary circle. 1362 found him at the court of Granada and when twenty years (and at least as many episodes) later he turned up in the Mamluk capital of Cairo, students flocked to his courses at the Azhar and he was appointed Maliki chief *qadi* of Cairo.

The great Spanish Sufi scholar, Ibn al-Arabi (d. 1240) wrote his *kitab al-Isra* in Fez. But, like most scholars, it was the pilgrimage that occasioned his most extensive travels. In 1202 he went to Mecca from Tunis, via Cairo and Jerusalem and two years later began to wend his way back through Baghdad and Mosul, Malatya and Konya.

Perhaps the most significant in this context is Ibn Battuta (1304-69) who came originally from Tangier but after thirty years of travels, which extended from China in the East to Spain and the Niger in the West, finally settled in Fez. There, under Merinid patronage he wrote an account of his travels. In these we learn that he so ingratiated himself with the Sultan of India, he was made chief *qadi* of Delhi and was later sent as his ambassador to China. It would, however, be too much to say that seven thousand miles from home Ibn Battuta encountered not a single cultural barrier, unless one understands this to mean there were no barriers to his gracious reception and promotion.

Ibn Battuta's travels began with the *haj*, but whether Africanus ever actually reached Mecca is open to debate. His itineraries are hard to follow and deal mainly with the Maghreb and the Niger which he visited with his uncle. Later he was captured by pirates in the Mediterranean and sent to Rome. It was for his new patron, Pope Leo, that he wrote his account. In Rome the young man from Fez agreed to be baptised and enjoyed considerable celebrity. But neither travel, exile nor conversion seems to have shaken his attachment to Islamic values. He ended his account by insisting, with a total disregard for his patron's sensibilities, that he would return 'unto mine own country'. And eventually, like Ibn Battuta, this is precisely what he did.

In 1972, after eleven years as a diplomat in the capitals of the West, Abdelmalek Tazi also returned to Fez. His decision was prompted less by nostalgia than by a conscious desire to extend the benefits and assurances or, as he puts it, to 'transmit the message' of his society, to his children. The French words he uses to describe this message – 'ambiance', 'culture', 'milieu' – are painfully inadequate. If they do justice to what remains of the traditional society in today's Fez it is a measure of how, as in other Arab cities, it has changed first under the pressures of colonialism, and then of tourism and commerce with the West.

Like many of his contemporaries Abdelmalek Tazi is drawn in different directions. He cherishes the social ideals imbibed as a child and still mirrored in the groundplan of the *medina*; but it was to the 'nouvelle ville' that he returned in 1972 and he appreciates the less inhibited and more challenging society of the West. He speaks fondly of Quranic school, yet sends his own children to the lycée. He respects the learning and craftsmanship on which Fez's reputation rested, yet he is now an industrialist who manufactures leather goods using the latest imported technology and European supervision.

In short he concedes that the traditional Muslim urban life has changed. But there are aspects of its society which are still relevant and none more so than its cosmopolitanism. Had Abdelmalek Tazi fulfilled his father's wish and become a member of the *ulama*, there is a sense in which he would have fulfilled the letter and not the spirit of a commitment to cultural tradition. This is so because the universal Islamic society in which the *ulama* flourished has been replaced by a new one in which Abdelmalek Tazi is well-qualified to engage.

His ultimate return to old Fez is yet to come. He and his brothers and uncles consider restoring the Tazi palace; what they would then do with it is less clear. But for Abdelmalek, as for most people, the memory of origin and of father are inseparable and pull hard against the currents:

81

(He left the *medina*) for his children, but every day, without exception, my father was going back to the *medina* to spend his day. He went down from nine to one o'clock. He came home to have lunch and then he started off again from three to late in the evening – every day. All his friends and relatives were there, all his relations even in business. He was used to going to the same mosque, for instance. He had to go to that mosque and not another one. Until he died – for more than twenty-five years, he was going every day back to the *medina*. So maybe because of that I have to come – to come back also.

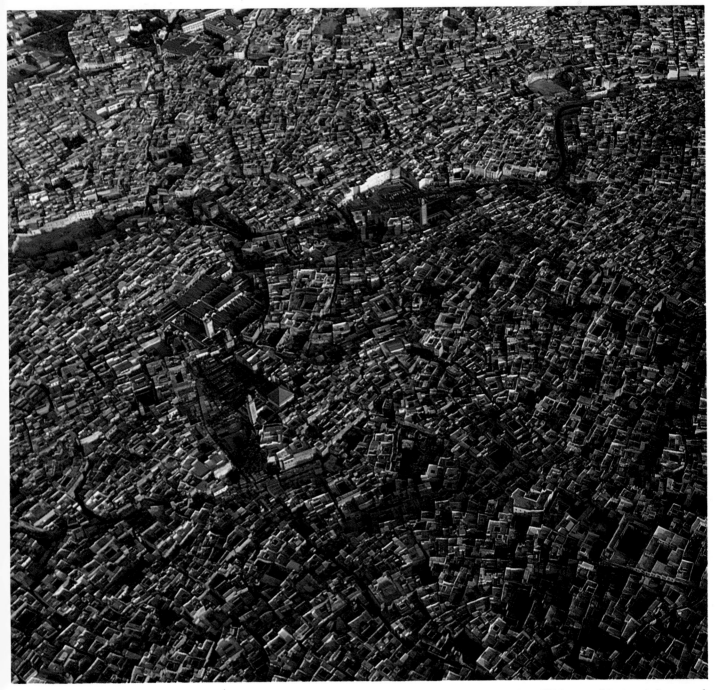

1. Fez, Morocco. The parallel green-tiled roofs of the mosque can be seen just left of centre, the pyramidal green roof of the 'madrassah' below it, and the river winding across the upper part of the picture.

Fez is the best preserved of medieval Islamic cities. Huddled around the two Jami, or Friday, mosques, its abutting houses and narrow lanes testify to the solidarity of the urban Islamic community and the interdependence of all its members. 'Believer is to believer,' declared the Prophet, 'as the mutually upholding sections of a building.'

2. *Qarawiyin Mosque, 12th century, Fez, Morocco*

The principal of Fez's two Jami mosques is the Qarawiyin (2). For the noon prayers on Friday the entire community both within and without the walls (3) gathered within its precincts. It thus served as both forum and cathedral. It was also a renowned centre of learning, attracting scholars and pupils from all over North Africa. Visiting students might stay in neighbouring 'khans' (inns) or in 'madrassah' (4), some of which had their own teaching staff as well as a place of prayer and residential halls.

3. *Bab el Makina, 18th century,*
leading into the medina of Fez

4. *Madrassah Attarine, 1323,*
Fez, Morocco

5. Dye vats in the tanneries, Fez, Morocco

6. (right) View into the metalware souk, Fez, Morocco

Around the Qarawiyin mosque was located the 'qisariya' or commercial centre of the city. To its souks the products of the city and the imported wares of the wholesaler were sent for retailing. The manufacture of jewellery, metalware (6) and piece goods was conducted in the immediate vicinity. More anti-social industries like tanning (5), dyeing, and milling were located beside the river and downstream of the city centre. They were still, however, within the walls. Likewise each trade had its own association akin to a guild but these too operated under a religious sanction, each having its own local mosque and being subject to the regulation of a religious official.

7. (top left) A street in the 'qisariya' of Fez

8. (top right) A tailor in the 'qisariya' of F[

9. (bottom left) A young boy works with a peen-ball hammer on brass trays, Fez

10. (bottom right) A cobbler, Fez, Morocco

Urban craftsmen contributed greatly to the celebrity of the city. Fez was famed for its saddlery and thread (as well as its hats), Mosul a[
Damascus for their inlaid metalwork (Damascene). The technical and artistic flair lavished on comparatively humble materials – gla[
ceramics, bronze and leather – to produce comparatively prosaic utensils – trays, candlesticks, jars, lamps – attests to the extent of the bourge[
or mercantile patronage alongside that of the princely court. This division of patronage is reflected in Fez in the physical distinction between t[
royal city centred on the palace (Fez Djid) and the commercial city centred on the Qarawiyin mosque (the medina).

11.
Candle-
stick, Iran,
late 14th
century

12.
Apothe-
cary's jar,
Syrian
Raqqa-
ware, 14th
century

13.
Mosque
lamp,
Syria or
Egypt,
14th
century

14. Bayt al-Sihaym, 1648-1796, Cairo, Egypt. View of one of the main reception rooms. Wooden screens or 'mashrabiyah' admit sunlight of an interior garden but not dust

The place of the Jami mosque as the religious and social heart of the city is repeated at a domestic level in the central courtyard in each household. Surrounded by a pillared cloister and verandahs the courtyard is where the family assembles for prayer just as the mosque is where the whole urban community prays. The head of the family leads the prayers just as the 'imam' does in the mosque.

Like the city each house presents a blank and forbidding wall on the outside; architectural and decorative extravagance is reserved in both house and mosque for the interior façades of the courtyard, the place of assembly and prayer.

15. House of Mohammed Lazake, 17th century, Fez, Morocco

In most Arab cities the royal palace together with the secretariat, treasury and barracks formed a distinct unit separate from the corporate life [of] the city. The city was thus to some extent inured to dynastic upheavals. Hence the remarkable continuity of social, intellectual and commercial life.

Most famous of the palace complexes of Western Islam is the Alhambra of Granada. Built between the twelfth and fourteenth centuries [its] nexus of courts, baths, mosques, gardens, barracks and stables is typically Islamic as is the elaborate ornamentation. But the impression [of] seclusion given by the smaller courtyards and proliferating loggias is less typical of early Muslim palaces where interior courtyards are on [a] semi-public scale.

17. Alhambra, view into the
Court of Lions

18. The Mirador Daraxa (Dar A'isha) in the Alhambra. The central medallion bears the verses of the poet Ibn Zamrak

19. Alhambra, the Fountain of the Generalife

CHAPTER FIVE

CITY
AND
COUNTRYSIDE

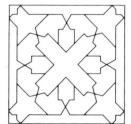 At this time we hear astonishing things about conditions in Cairo and Egypt as regards luxury and wealth in the customs of the inhabitants there. Indeed many of the poor in Maghreb want to move to Egypt on account of that and because they hear that prosperity in Egypt is greater than anywhere else.

When Ibn Khaldun (1332-1406) wrote the *Muqaddimah* (Introduction) to his *Universal History* (*Kitab al-'Ibar*) he was living near Oran in what is now Algeria. He had just fallen from favour with the Merinids in Fez and was enjoying a sabbatical interlude of scholarship before himself succumbing to Cairo's gravitational pull. Without as yet having seen Egypt he accepted its wealth as beyond question. But he had his own explanation for it. Whatever the people of the Maghreb might think, Cairo and Egypt were rich because conditions there conformed exactly to those which he had formulated as being conducive to wealth and civilisation the world over.

The common people [of the Maghreb] believe that [Egypt is prosperous] because property is abundant in those regions, and their inhabitants have much property stored away, and are more charitable and bountiful than the inhabitants of any other city. However, this is not so but, as one knows, the reason is that the population of Egypt and Cairo is larger than that of any other city one can think of.

Cairo was one of the world's largest cities and in fact, as well as by Ibn Khaldun's definition, one of the wealthiest. He called it the 'metropolis of the universe, the garden of the world, the swarming core of the human species'. At almost any date before the present century a direct relationship did exist between population and prosperity; and nowhere was this more in evidence and more crucial than beside the lower Nile, the most densely peopled area in the Arab world.

The Arabic word that Ibn Khaldun used for 'population' was '*umran*'. It derives from a root meaning 'to grow' or 'develop' and he used precisely the same word to signify 'civilisation'. In Ibn Khaldun's theory of history, population growth was therefore inseparable from the concept of civilised life. The more people, the more wealth, the more civilisation. When society consisted solely of Bedouin tribes all available labour had to be concentrated on producing the bare necessities of existence. But if such a society, under the leadership of a powerful dynasty, selected a favourable site for settlement and then grew beyond mere self-sufficiency, it entered a wealth-creating phase. Those citizens freed of the drudgery of agriculture could engage in trade, industry and the civilising arts. Luxury and leisure followed; and, in time, decadence too.

A glance at Egypt and Cairo today might suggest that the great Maghrebi historian had got it all terribly wrong. Far from creating wealth or sustaining civilisation, today's over-population is seen as having condemned Egyptians to chronic poverty, desperate over-crowding and frantic migration. Even in the late fourteenth century Cairo was not quite as 'astonishing' as Ibn Khaldun had heard. The Black Death had just swept through the city and the Mongols under Tamerlane were poised to do the same. The city's medieval zenith under Saladin's successors and under the early Mamelukes was past.

Ibn Khaldun's theories were based on his experience of cities like Tunis and Fez. He contrasted their patterns of existence with that of their surrounding desert and its semi-nomadic Berber and Bedouin population. But he had very little to say about what might be considered as an intermediate life-style, that of the peasant farmer. In Egypt, unlike in the Maghreb, most of the population was engaged in farming. Society here therefore had three components, desert, countryside and city, and it was on a balanced relationship between the last two that growth, prosperity and civilisation depended.

A basic pattern existed from the earliest times. Cultivation and urban settlement made their first appearance in delta regions like those of the Nile and the Tigris/Euphrates where riverine flooding left basins of low-lying land suitably watered and enriched. But the disadvantage of delta regions was that they were notoriously hard to defend, standing crops were tempting and sedentary life was vulnerable. To keep off marauding nomads the agricultural community looked to the city as the centre of government and protection. If this was forthcoming, agriculture flourished and a surplus was generated for supporting and expanding the city. Put another way, the prosperity of the city depended on its ability to exercise effective and equitable control over the countryside. There was also a straight commercial equation; the countryside needed the city as a market for its surplus and the city needed the countryside as a market for its basic manufactures.

The arrival in the Nile valley of an Arab army in AD 640 did not change this basic pattern. As a new source of protection the Arabs replaced the Byzantines and their encampment on the east bank of the Nile, Fustat, replaced Babylon – and a host of earlier centres going back to Memphis – as the urban nucleus. Fustat, meaning 'an entrenched camp', was soon a city with its Jami Masjid and commercial centre but here, as in Fez, subsequent dynasties signified their authority by constructing new urban units rather than just expanding the old. In 750 the Abbasids founded Al-Askar, in 1870 Ahmad Ibn Tulun founded Al-Qita'i (the only remnant of which is the magnificent Ibn Tulun mosque) and in 969 the Fatimids built Al-Qahira (Cairo), the City Victorious. In each case the new city was somewhat to the north of its predecessor; Cairo was edging downstream but always on the east bank, that nearest to the Arab and Islamic heartland. Behind it there accumulated a trail of structures which in time became ruins. Already the city had acquired extravagant tastes in the matter of land appropriation.

Of Cairo's founder figures the only one to go against this trend was the great Salah-al-Din (Saladin 1169-1193). Exhibiting in this, as in his political career, a remarkably modest and practical bent, he built no new city but consolidated the old. By expanding the Fatimid Al-Qahira to make it the commercial as well as the royal capital, by adding to the south of it his massive Citadel as a central barracks and power base, and by planning the first fortifications to encompass the entire nexus of cities, he more than anyone determined the identity of Cairo and defined its totality as it was to remain for the next six hundred years. There were some further additions both inside and outside the walls but Cairo was now one city and increasingly referred to as such.

One of the primary facts of Egyptian history in late medieval times is that of a general depopulation, which resulted in a severe reduction in the area of cultivated land and agricultural production. After the Black Death (1348), the great plague of the fourteenth century, epidemics struck the life of every generation until the nineteenth century. Late medieval historians and chroniclers recorded the wholesale abandonment of villages. Ibn Khaldun had no doubts about the central importance of demographic decline ('Civilisation decreased with the decrease of mankind.')

In the middle of the eighth [fourteenth] century, civilisation both in the East and the West was visited by a destructive plague which devastated nations and caused populations to vanish. It swallowed up many of the good things of civilisation and wiped them out. . . . Civilisation decreased with the decrease of mankind. Cities and buildings were laid waste, roads and way signs were obliterated, settlements and mansions became empty, dynasties and tribes grew weak. The entire inhabited world changed. . . . It was as if the voice of existence in the world had called out for oblivion and restriction, and the world had responded to its call.

In 1434 there were only just over 2,000 villages in Egypt compared to 10,000 in the tenth century. From a high of perhaps eight million it has been estimated that the population of the whole country fell to just three million by 1800. This had serious consequences for Cairo. Urban death rates were always well above urban birth rates and the city traditionally depended on the countryside for people as well as for food. Between 1500 and 1800 the population of Cairo was halved – from perhaps 500,000 to 250,000. The historian Magrizi described whole quarters of Cairo lying in ruin or abandoned at the beginning of the fifteenth century. Seventeenth-century accounts of 'the metropolis of the universe' describe the streets as choked by rubble, the canals dried up, the lakes festering and the whole city rimmed by mountains of compost. In the countryside marginal lands were deserted, public works neglected and irrigation schemes abandoned. In the course of three centuries the richest city in the world had become synonymous with oriental 'decadence'.

* * *

Egyptians call Cairo 'Misr'; it's the word by which they also know Egypt. Today, more than ever, Cairo *is* Egypt, the home of one-fifth of the entire Egyptian population. Pressed to articulate his reasons for leaving home and going to Cairo, Mitwali, a young peasant from the Delta village of Dahria, couches his replies in stubborn defiance.

'It's the digging, the watering, the ploughing. I've had enough of farming.'

Life in his village is hard but not unbearably so. For Mitwali the 'push' from the countryside is not so much deprivation as drudgery – the spadework and the waterwheel. As for the city he has few illusions about the easy life. If he is lucky enough to find work the hours will be long and the pay little; food and rent will account for most of it. And he will live with several other migrants from his village; it is not a question of escaping from a restrictive community. Why then does he go?

'The streets, the cinema, the zoo, everything.'

There is nothing peculiarly Egyptian about Mitwali's obsession with the city. It is shared by many young peasant farmers in every Third World country. Migration is no longer simply a reaction to local economic factors. Mitwali's expectations are of an order that would never have occurred to Ibn Khaldun; they have been generated by an awareness of a contemporary acquisitive and immensely attractive life-style, that of the modern city.

The city by which Mitwali is so beguiled is not the Fatimid capital, nor the walled metropolis of Saladin, but a modern creation of the nineteenth century. The great transformation of Egypt in the nineteenth century was the significant achievement of Ismail Pasha's grandfather, Mohammed Ali, the founder of modern Egypt. Napoleon invaded Egypt in 1798 and controlled it for three years, enough to jolt Egyptian society without influencing it in any deep way. Mohammed Ali had come to Egypt as commander of an Albanian contingent in the Ottomans' counter-invasion force in 1801. When the country was restored to Istanbul the Albanians were a power to reckon with in

Cairo. After the inevitable struggle their leader was able to demand for himself the pashalik. Mohammed Ali knew full well the weakness of his suzerains but he was also aware that Egypt itself was no longer a secure power base. His aim therefore was not just to rule but to transform the country.

Helped by his capable son Ibrahim and by his own unusually long reign – forty-three years – he launched one of the most ambitious modernisation programmes ever undertaken by a non-colonial power. It included re-establishing law and order, reorganising the entire government, creating an effective military machine and interesting the Egyptians themselves in soldiering. It included establishing colleges of higher and technical education, setting up factories and establishing a policy for industrial development, all with the help of hired European advisers. But above all it was an agrarian revolution. Mohammed Ali appreciated that however dominant Cairo might be in Egyptian life, its prosperity, that of the government and that of the nation depended on the land. Almost alone amongst Egypt's recent rulers he put the countryside before the city.

Not that this meant any coddling of the *fellahin* (peasants). Quite the opposite. The system of land tenure was reformed, abolishing the feudal amirs and substituting a state monopoly of all agricultural land. According to members of Napoleon's expedition only one-fifth of the taxes levied on the cultivator had previously reached the treasury. Now, under Mohammed Ali, the land tax alone supplied half the government's total revenue.

Likewise the extensive improvements in irrigation, communications, crop rotation and seed. Dams were rebuilt, old canals cleaned out, new ones cut, marginal lands reclaimed and, in the Delta, perennial irrigation (permitting more than one crop a year) became the norm. This last was essential for the success of his most celebrated innovation, the introduction of long-staple cotton. Within a decade Egypt became one of the world's major cotton producers and cotton became one of the country's major sources of revenue. It was grown during the summer season when the fields without perennial irrigation would normally have been fallow.

One aspect of Egypt's transformation stands out. In the nineteenth century the long-term demographic decline of Egypt was reversed and its population entered a new phase of steady and, later, vigorous growth. Egypt's population of about three million in 1798 did not begin its steady upward acceleration until about 1840. At the end of Ismail's reign, the population had reached seven million, a doubling in forty years. (Such rates of increase are unknown outside Europe before the twentieth century.) The pattern had been established, and it continued: at the end of the nineteenth century the population exceeded nine million.

Major upheavals in the very structure of the Egyptian economy had preceded and accompanied the population expansion. The revolution in the system of land tenure and the introduction of cotton radically changed agricultural and social relations and affected all Egyptians. The changes in the system of land tenure resulted in the creation of a new class of large landowners and turned the majority of the Egyptian peasants into either tenant farmers or labourers. The cultivation of cotton is a labour-intensive industry, and in the first half of the nineteenth century, before the full recovery from the demographic depression of the previous centuries, Egypt suffered from a labour shortage, which held back cotton production. As more and more acreage was devoted to cotton, the demand for labour increased. Children and women filled this demand.

To facilitate economic planning the government of Mohammed Ali established a monopoly not only of cotton but of practically all other crops. Mohammed Ali's rule was a classic example of what is now called a managed economy. It was also autocratic, authoritarian, repressive and efficient. If anything it worked too well. The success of Mohammed Ali's forces occupying Syria in the 1830s provoked the hostility of the Ottoman government and of its British ally; the success of cotton ultimately made the economy dangerously dependent on fluctuations in the world market; and the system of state monopolies and price fixing antagonised European buyers and merchant houses.

In 1836-7 cotton prices slumped and the shortfall in revenue was made good by disposing of agricultural land to officials and members of the royal family. A form of agrarian revolt followed and in the 1840s an unholy alliance of the Ottoman Empire, the British, foreign business houses and rural shaikhs (or tax-gatherers) forced Mohammed Ali to abandon his monopolies. By another curious irony the man who had done most to modernise Egypt became the man responsible for legitimising the great agricultural estates, including those of the royal family, which were to bedevil efforts at land reform until the mid-twentieth century, and for opening the door to foreign investment and direct manipulation of the rural economy by foreign business.

It was during the reign of Abbas I (1848-54) that steps were taken which had the effect of firmly connecting Cairo to the new world system of mechanised transportation. In addition to the improvement of road communications between Cairo and Suez, Robert Stephenson built (1852-4) the first railway between Cairo and Alexandria, which cut the time of travel between Cairo and Egypt's seaport on the Mediterranean from four days to four and a half hours. But in terms of Egypt's place in the world system, the single most important event was the responsibility of Abbas's successor, Sa'id (1854-63) who, in

November 1854, granted de Lesseps the concession to construct the Suez Canal. The physical condition of the city of Cairo itself, however, still awaited change.

Ismail Pasha paid attention to urban development from the moment he became ruler of Egypt in 1863. His era remains the historically decisive one for the modern city of Cairo. In 1867 he headed a massive Egyptian delegation to the Exposition Universelle in Paris. The Exposition marked the climax of Baron Haussman's work in replanning Paris and Ismail was profoundly impressed by all he saw. In two years' time he was to open the Suez Canal in what was to be Egypt's own 'Exposition'. How better to declare Egypt 'a part of Europe' than by doing for Cairo what Haussman had done for Paris? Whatever Ismail's other failings, he was no procrastinator; most of the city was planned and built in just two years. In Ali Mubarak, his remarkable Minister of Public Works, he found the right man for the job. Luckily there was no call for wholesale demolition. In preceding centuries the bed of the Nile had been shifting slowly west. A tract of wasteland now intervened between the city and the river and it was here, facing west, that the indefatigable Ali Mubarak laid out the grand façade of boulevards, parks and *étoiles* that was to be Ismail's Cairo. Like Egypt itself, the city was 'the gift of the Nile'.

In November 1869 the Canal was opened. The crowned heads of Europe, the world's press, the entrepreneurs and the pundits came to Cairo looking for oriental mystery. They were confronted with occidental elegance. *Rigoletto* was being performed at the new Opera House, the street lighting was on, the National Theatre was open, rolling acres of wasteland were being transformed into wooded parkland with grottoes and belvederes, a road had been built to conduct the visitors to the Pyramids and, for the first time, a bridge had been thrown across the Nile, thus inaugurating the city's expansion to the west bank. Cairo had, literally, turned its back on the East. Ismail himself, resplendent with insignia, epaulettes and drooping moustache, looked like a European, and perhaps even thought like a European. It is tempting to see his Cairo as a simple, even superficial, imitation of Haussman's Paris. But then, new Cairo was equally, and perhaps more accurately, Ali Mubarak's Cairo. As such it acquires new meaning.

Ali Mubarak was born in 1824; he died in 1893. He came from a peasant family in the Egyptian delta, was trained in Mohammed Ali's state schools, sent to Paris to be trained as a military engineer, came back to Egypt in 1850, and between 1850 and 1882 – that is, until the British Occupation – was the most important civil servant in Egypt. He was Minister of Education, of Public Works, and of Railroads (note that Egypt had a railroad in 1853, which is more than can be said for Sweden or Japan).

Between 1868 and 1872 the man who planned new Cairo wrote extensively to tell us why he was doing it the way he was. He wrote about modernity and tradition, explained why he built streets the way he did, why he knocked down old monuments. He explored the difference between Cairo and Alexandria, on the one hand, and Paris and Marseilles, on the other. His writings deserve notice because they make articulate the ideas current among the new ruling group of Egypt and which underlay the reforms of the age of Ismail. Mubarak believed in science, progress, civilisation, planning, machines and in public service. In short he was, if a label is needed, a kind of utilitarian, a true son of the promise and optimism of the nineteenth century. The growth of knowledge, in his opinion, was the single most important reason for the advance of the Europeans to the forefront of all civilised communities.

Europeans, Mubarak insisted, would never have achieved this power and influence had they restricted themselves to their original basic ideas and the ancient knowledge of their forefathers. In its own age of greatness, Islam was comparable to modern Europe and for precisely the same reasons: knowledge, science and borrowing. The Europeans borrowed from the Arabs, the Arabs from the ancients, and the ancients from the ancient Egyptians. He then adds that even the ancient Egyptians must have had precursors from whom they borrowed. The negation of borrowing is isolation, and isolation is the very mark of backwardness, the condition of the precivilised and the barbarian.

There was a mood of expansive optimism in Egypt as the country apparently leapt from the Middle Ages to the forefront of nineteenth-century progress. The harvest of Mohammed Ali's reform programme was, in time, considerable, and Ali Mubarak was a living example of that harvest. But without direct control over the revenue from the countryside, and without the alternative of a thriving industrial base, the foundations of modern Egypt remained weak. During the latter half of the century the population, which in the 1820s had been considered inadequate for the new intensified farming, doubled and the agricultural surplus also doubled; during the American Civil War the value of the cotton crop actually quadrupled. But the dispersal of land also continued and, by the time it reached the treasury, agrarian revenue was pitifully depleted. With each economic set-back, with each heavily subsidised 'modernisation', and with each royal extravagance, the state sank deeper into debt. Larger loans meant recourse to European bankers and the price of each loan became a concession to European interests. Soon new loans were required just to service the old. With a dreary inevitability Egypt defaulted, the resultant Anglo-French receivership was threatened by a nationalist uprising and, in 1882, British colonial rule was imposed by force.

When the British occupied the country in 1882, Egypt had already been undergoing, for seventy-five years, a fundamental transformation in its land, economy, agriculture and population. The difference between Egypt and any of the other slabs of pink on the imperial map was that this was a country which had already been through the traumas of modernisation. Under British rule the irrigation network would be further extended in the Delta, the first Aswan dams would be built and perennial irrigation would be extended to Upper Egypt. Cotton would continue to flourish and communications to be improved. But there was nothing new in all this. It was a quantitive change, not qualitative. The point is well illustrated by Ismail's sensational transformation of Cairo. In India it was not until 1911 that the British decided to build a modern, European-style capital; and it was a further twenty years before New Delhi was inaugurated. In Egypt 'new Cairo' was ready and waiting in 1882.

After the British occupation of Egypt, the rise of a man like Ali Mubarak was no longer possible because no Egyptian could occupy a position of true responsibility. If a dam was built on the Nile it was not an Egyptian but an Englishman who made the decision. For a few critical generations, Egyptians were not allowed to rule or to assume any responsible role in their own country, and this was the hidden and heavy price of imperialism for the Middle East. The difficulties which the new nations of the Arab and Third Worlds have had are directly related to the gap that imperialism caused in the succession of responsibility for the affairs of their own societies.

*   *   *

The phenomenal growth of Cairo under Ismail was not matched by a corresponding increase in population, at least not immediately. The new city was not designed for rural immigrants and imminent bankruptcy was no incentive to migration. But during the first decade of British rule economic prospects improved. Priority was given to agriculture with new irrigation schemes, and further encouragement of cotton. Land revenue improved, the population as a whole climbed steeply and with it migration to the city revived. Ibn Khaldun would have recognised the pattern. By 1907 Cairo had 600,000 inhabitants including a growing foreign community (of mainly Europeans and Turks). A further increment resulted from the absorption of neighbouring villages into the city, most notably on the west bank of the Nile. This process of the city gobbling up the surrounding countryside and transforming villages into suburbs would remain a feature of Cairo's growth and give the city a unique character.

But neither the absorption of neighbouring villages nor even migration alone can account for the population explosion which now took place. In a decade Cairo's population nearly doubled. It passed the one million mark in 1927, by 1947 it was over two million, by 1967 it was five million and today greater Cairo is estimated at ten million (give or take an error factor which is now probably larger than the total population in Ismail's day). For the first time the growth rate of the city exceeded that of the country as a whole, a possibility which would never have occurred to Ibn Khaldun. But then neither would the explanation; what triggered the population explosion, in Cairo as in so many cities, was the dramatic reduction in mortality rates that came with sanitation and medical facilities.

If cleanliness was next to godliness, then for the British empire-builders plumbing ranked as a moral imperative, indeed a civilising art. The cess-pit was the breeding ground of vice as well as of cholera and mosquitos; Cairo, which had never known any other method of waste disposal, must have a sewerage system. Between 1915 and 1920 fifty kilometres of drains were laid with pumping stations and purification plants. Instantly the age-old problem of city deaths far exceeding city births was reversed. It has been estimated that about half the increase in the city's population was directly attributable to this innovation.

Vaccination and basic health care were to have equally dramatic effects. But these were not peculiar to the city. In the countryside the population was also experiencing unprecedented growth – so much so that the steady process of land reclamation was unable to keep pace, average land holdings shrank to less than an acre (though the top 1% of landlords actually increased their holdings) and the flow of migrants to the city rose to a deluge. In the middle of the twentieth century the population of Egypt reached twenty-seven million – an eightfold increase over the beginning of the previous century. Nowadays, with a population of over forty million, Egypt is believed to have a problem of overpopulation, and it is easy to forget that in the last century Egypt's problem was underpopulation.

* * *

By 1980 when Mitwali, the boy from Dharia, arrived in Cairo he found a city one-third of whose residents were, like him, migrants from the countryside. (In that year alone about 100,000 newcomers settled in Cairo.) The sparse cell that Mitwali was lucky enough to occupy delighted him. It had electric light and he shared it with only two others, a room occupancy rate well below the city's average. True, there was only one bed but they slept in it by shifts. The room was in what economists call high-rise, high density, low income housing. It was situated in Cairo's northern suburbs which, following the mid-century introduction of the tram, quadrupled the city's area. Thanks to his job Mitwali could afford to see the occasional film, to visit the zoo and the coffee house and to roam the city. He discarded the gallabiya for shirt and trousers. They felt good. He was happy; he had apparently leaped a cultural barrier without mishap.

But this impression is misleading. For one thing it is uncertain whether Mitwali and the millions of other peasant migrants are being urbanised or whether Cairo is being ruralised. The city continues to devour the surrounding countryside but is it assimilating it? Urban villages obstinately retain something of their distinctive character and even the high-rise monstrosities are not the dehumanising structures of the West. The incomers tend to settle in specific areas – near the railway and bus termini or around the outskirts; and those from the same village or those who share the same trade tend to congregate in particular neighbourhoods, to patronise the same coffee houses and to set up mutual aid associations. Neither alienation nor, conversely, social mobility, is a concomitant of urban residence. Just as the old city was divided into quarters each of which was originally settled by people from the same tribe or area, so the new city is creating its own cellular structure. The flood of migrants could yet bring city and countryside closer together, or rather, blur the age-old dichotomy between the two.

In another sense, though, quite the opposite is happening. Mitwali, like the majority of incomers, found work in the service sector; he washed cars. In spite of heroic endeavours during the Nasser revolution, Egypt's industrial sector remains more capital intensive than labour intensive. Employment of a productive nature is hard to find, especially for the unskilled. For Dr Galal Amin, an economist at the American University of Cairo, the big difference between the Third World city and its Western counterpart is that the former is a consumer city, the latter a producer city. Without a modern manufacturing base, Cairo has grown on trade, government, and exploitation of the countryside. The encouragement of cash crops like cotton and sugar means that the city no longer guarantees consumption of the rural surplus. Instead it disposes of it on the world markets, and then imports whatever it fancies in the way of consumer items.

'I am inclined to think of all this as an act of economic betrayal of the village by the city,' says Dr Amin. 'But to this act of betrayal I would add another which to my mind is far more serious. For just at the time when the city started to import consumer goods from the West it also started to import Western value systems and ways of thinking.'

This last was 'a cultural betrayal'. Its calamitous results can be traced both in the crumbling structure of Old Cairo and in the unashamedly imitative aspirations of the likes of Mitwali. Cultural interaction should be beneficial but in such a hopelessly unequal partnership, adaptation tends to be hasty and indiscriminate. It was true in Ismail's day and it is even more true today. The independent Arab states may pay lip service to socialism, pan-Arabism or nationalism, but it makes little difference. In the past twenty-five years, though starting from vastly different social and economic conditions and though pursuing a variety of ideologies, they have shown remarkable consistency in affecting the trappings of Western modernity with scant regard for the consequences. Only Nasser, with his emphasis on national regeneration, agricultural reform and import substitution, attempted to tackle the problem. But, like Mohammed Ali before him, he was forced by military defeat and outside economic pressure to abandon the experiment before it bore fruit. The only modernisation programme that has been successfully realised throughout the Arab world has been 'the modernisation of poverty'.

Surprisingly Dr Galal Amin does not consider himself a prophet of doom. He has confidence in the resilience of traditional Arab values and, in Egypt's case, he has confidence in the country's two natural resources – land and people. The construction of the Aswan High Dam in the 1960s at last brought complete control of the Nile waters. Perennial irrigation is now possible throughout both Upper and Lower Egypt. To some extent this has been offset by salination and leaching, especially in the Delta. But given better drainage and soil conservation the country could once again be poised for an agricultural surge. Galal Amin believes that in a renewed commitment to the welfare of the countryside, in a diversion of funds and expertise to agriculture, lies Egypt's best chance of reversing the effects of cultural and economic betrayal. The strength to resist must come from within.

Mitwali, eventually if reluctantly, went back to his village. The decision was forced upon him by his family and his price for returning was to be excused from farm work. Instead he was apprenticed to a village tailor. By producing gallabiyas for the villagers of Dharia, Mitwali is contributing to the self-sufficiency of the rural community and to the diffusion of basic technology. But like many other returning migrants he is also contributing to the urbanisation of the village. He has become fond of television; he expects his home to have electricity. Increasingly such expectations are being realised thanks to a new phenomenon – emigration. In 1973 perhaps 100,000 Egyptians were working abroad; ten years later a figure of three million is projected. The emigrants are no longer the elite – academics and professional men – but skilled, semi-skilled and even unskilled. Invariably their destinations are Saudi Arabia and the oil-rich Gulf states. The construction boom which followed the upsurge in oil prices in 1973-4 has sparked off a movement of labour within the Arab world of mammoth proportions and unforeseeable consequences.

Egypt with the largest labour surplus leads the table of labour exporting states. At Cairo airport scenes reminiscent of the gold rush are enacted. An average of 3000 hopefuls a day board eastward flights thus dramatically easing pressures at home. On the same day nearly as many – for most labour contracts are temporary – return laden with the spoils of exile. Videos and hi-fis, televisions and cameras litter the airport foyer. And these are only the tip of the iceberg. From a vast balance of payments deficit in the mid-1970s Egypt had moved into surplus by 1980, thanks largely to some $2,000 million a year being remitted home by migrant workers.

Whether this vast influx of capital will merely push up domestic inflation or whether it can be channelled into productive investment remains to be seen. But then so do all the other effects of emigration. Are, for instance, the spoils of the Gulf satisfying or merely fanning those expectations which Galal Amin decries? Is the villager who returns with boxes of consumer gadgetry and the money to buy a new house enriching village life or impoverishing it? And will Mitwali remain bent over the sewing machine now that there is a video next door? Or will he too sucumb to the allure of the Gulf? How long will the boom last and what happens when it is over? Like Ibn Khaldun retreating to formulate his theory of history, it is a good moment to reconsider the relationship of city and countryside, of population and prosperity, in a desperately one-sided world.

2. *The Nile Delta near Rashid*

3. *Mitwali Balah at the railway station in Tanta on the Nile Delta*

For people, as for provisions, Cairo has traditionally depended on the fertile and densely populated Nile Valley. But in modern times the urban population has itself registered a significant natural increase. This, however, has not discouraged immigration from the countryside. There too the ever diminishing size of landholdings has been hastened by higher fertility rates plus an increasing dependence on cash crops, like cotton, whose value fluctuates on a world market beyond even national control. Forced to consider migrating from his land the peasant is also tempted by the allure of city life as portrayed in the media and perceived in the arrival of consumer goods in the village. The railway to Cairo has been there for over a hundred years; but the forces which impel ever more Egyptian peasants to buy a one-way ticket to Cairo are of new and irresistible persuasion.

To most Egyptians Cairo is 'Misr', the word they also use for Egypt. It is already the home of more than a quarter of the country's entire population and is still growing. The traditional but precarious economic and demographic equilibrium between the city and the countryside has been destroyed with alarming consequences for both.

Cairo, view over Abdel el Meneim Square

5. *A camel market on the outskirts of Cairo*

Population pressures in Cairo now rank with those of Calcutta. In spite of new satellite cities and heroic redevelopment programmes, the new housing is woefully inadequate and the old often unsafe. On the eastern fringes of the city the acres of mausolea known as the City of the Dead (6) have been reinhabited – though not rehabilitated – by a living population of more than 100,000, most of whom will have been born, will live and will die in a tomb.

6. *The City of the Dead, Cairo*

7. *(facing page, top) Freelance rubbish collectors, Ca*

8. *(facing page, bottom) Knife seller in Ca*

9. Immigrant dock workers in Jeddah, Saudi Arabia

10. Egyptian immigrant workers at Kuwait's international airport

No longer able or content to scratch a living from the land and yet frustrated by the city's failure to provide an alternative livelihood, more and more Egyptians entertain the idea of emigrating to the oil-rich Arab states. In the 1970s migration within the Arab world reached unprecedented levels with Egyptians, Yemenis, Jordanians and Palestinians heading the mass movement of labour to the capital-rich but labour-poor states of the Gulf, Libya and Saudi Arabia.

In the short term this contract labour offers obvious benefits to both the host nation and the donor nation (through remittances sent home). It may also intensify pan-Arab awareness and exchange. But it solves none of the underlying problems. In some of the Gulf states, where migrant workers account for 80% of the population, there is suspicion and resentment on both sides. In the donor countries themselves emigration is found not to drain off the unskilled labour surplus but to siphon away the precious cream of semi-skilled, skilled and professional workers. The problem comes full circle in Cairo where the construction of desperately needed housing is being held up because of the exodus of engineers and masons to the Gulf.

CHAPTER SIX

NEW KNOWLEDGE FOR OLD

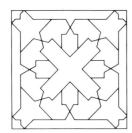 Thirty years ago Kuwait was a sleepy, mud-walled seaport best known for its pearl fisheries. Today, thanks to oil, it is a rich country, and the possessor of one of the leading research and development institutes in the Arab world. Here, at the Kuwait Institute of Scientific Research (KISR), important work is being done in marine biology and on the use of solar power for generating electricity. Recently an Arabic word-processor has been developed.

This achievement has not surprised its protagonists. But how does a traditional trading community produce computer specialists overnight? If outsiders remain sceptical, it is because they are convinced that KISR owes nothing to Kuwait except the cash. The technology and the equipment must be Japanese, American or European, and the personnel, even if they are Arabs by birth, must have been trained elsewhere. And this is indeed the case: it is an example of determined and unabashed appropriation. The scientists at KISR recognise no cultural chasms inhibiting the passage of ideas, nor any ethnic barriers to their further elaboration, and given Kuwait's extraordinary progress in the last three decades, they confidently anticipate that within another decade innovation will supersede appropriation. Having judiciously selected, mastered and synthesised the most relevant technologies, the Arabs will then be ready to take a scientific lead which will benefit not just themselves but mankind as a whole. This may sound like Third World romanticism – but after all, their ancestors have done it before.

*   *   *

Nothing better testifies to the vitality and confidence of early Islam than its willingness to learn from its subjects. Finding themselves the masters of an empire which embraced an extraordinary variety of cultural and scholarly traditions the Arabs, a people possessed of a rich literary tradition but with little in the way of scholarship, proceeded to investigate, synthesise and develop the scholarly largesse of their inheritance. This included Euclid, Hippocrates, Aristotle, Galen, Ptolemy and the neo-Platonists. It also included works of Persian and Indian origin. 'Shall those who have knowledge and those who have it not be deemed equal?' the Quran asked, rhetorically. 'The ink of scholars is

118

more valuable than the blood of martyrs,' declared the Prophet in a hadith which supplied the answer. For 'the search for knowledge is an obligation for every Muslim.' Few religions have placed such emphasis on the acquisition of learning and few societies have pursued it more vigorously. 'We should not be ashamed to acknowledge truth from whatever source it comes to us, even if it is brought to us by former generations and foreign peoples,' wrote al-Kindi (d. 873), one of the earliest Arab philosophers.

During the eighth and ninth centuries the first great systematic appropriation of learning in history took place. The immediate priority was the collection of manuscripts and their translation into Arabic. This was a formidable task, not least because the Arabic language had itself to be enlarged and refined to express the subtle concepts and the scientific terminology of the new learning. Translators often had to check several versions of the same text to identify a precise meaning and then to consult with lexicographers over its rendering into Arabic. This ambitious and painstaking undertaking needed powerful patronage if it was to be sustained, and under the Abbasid caliphs in their new capital of Baghdad it received just that. Al-Mamun (813-33) actually institutionalised the process in the famous Bayt al-Hikma, or Institute of Science, a library, translation bureau and research centre which acted as a clearing-house for all the foreign sciences.

Many of the great figures in this move to translate the key manuscripts were neither Arabs nor Muslims. The most famous, Hunayn Ibn Ishaq (d. 873), was a Nestorian Christian whose first language was Syriac. Others were Persians, or members of a pagan, Greek-speaking community in Mesopotamia known as the Sabaeans. The learning of the ancient world had long since been flushed from its traditional centres of Athens, Bzyantium and Alexandria and now survived in isolation and scattered fragments on the fringes of what had once been the classical world. Its guardians were Christians, Jews, Sabaeans and Zoroastrians who had already translated many works into Syriac and Pahlevi from the original Greek. They were also aware of other, non-Greek traditions of learning, especially those of Sassanian Persia and Gupta India. But the translation was now into Arabic, and Arabic henceforth became the language of the 'rational' sciences as it was of the 'religious'. Moreover, the process of appropriation was directed and sponsored by Arabs and was only possible because of the extent of Arab conquests. Had the Arabs played no further part in scientific enquiry, the fact that they had managed, for the first time in history, to assemble a truly comprehensive and universal corpus of human knowledge would justify the term 'Arabic science'.

The notion that that was the extent of it, that the Arabs – or rather, the Muslims – did no more than rescue the science and philosophy of the ancient world, uncritically adopt it, classify it, and then discard it until acquisitive Renaissance minds recognised its true value, is a European conceit long since discredited. Obviously, though, not all disciplines received equal attention and patronage. Some were of immediate and practical value to their sponsors. Medical study, for instance, offered the prospect of better health and better treatment. When the Caliph al-Mansur (754-75) fell ill he enquired for the best physician in his empire and was recommended to a Nestorian Christian, Jibra'il Ibn Baktishu, of Jundishapur in Persia. This man and his descendants subsequently served as court physicians to successive caliphs and thus the learning and expertise of the medical school in Jundishapur, the most advanced of its day, came to inspire Islamic medicine. Similarly, astrology received direct encouragement, princes being ever anxious about the future. Astronomy and astronomical and orological devices also had an important religious function; the precise bearing of Mecca and the exact time of the day are matters of vital consideration in the orientation and routine of prayer. Innovative and exact skills were devoted to the development of the quadrant and the astrolabe, precise observational and calculating instruments.

But, in the words of Abdelhamid Sabra, Professor of the History of Arabic Science at Harvard, 'the enterprise of Islamic science and philosophy, with its high level of achievement and its marked interest in theoretical and abstract questions, can hardly be explained as the unintended consequence of the practical concerns of a few individuals, however powerful and influential.'

In Islam, as in other civilisations, nothing less profound than genuine curiosity, or less complicated than the interplay of social, cultural and deep human needs can suffice to explain such an impressive and long-lasting enterprise.

Professor Sabra is a recognised authority on Ibn al-Haytham (known to European science as Alhazen), who was born in Basrah (Iraq) in 965 but who spent most of his life in Egypt. Like other Arabic scholars, Ibn al-Haytham appears something of a polymath by modern standards; his ninety-odd works include studies in philosophy, theology, astronomy, geometry, music and mathematics. He actually went to Egypt with a plan for regulating the waters of the Nile, but the work on which his celebrity in the West rests is entitled *On Optics*.

In this work, an attempt to understand the whole physical and psychological process of sight, Ibn al-Haytham combined the medical, mathematical and physical explanations of his predecessors and, by testing them and often radically reshaping them, arrived at a new theory of vision which, in the opinion of Professor Sabra, 'was richer and more sophisticated than all previous theories'. He distinguished light and colour as the two physical properties of a given object which, emanating from it, are received by the eye. He elaborated the geometry by which the eye converts the image and the psychology by which the brain interprets the eye's message, giving the object size, shape and distance. Apart from its sophisticated mathematics and remarkably advanced formulation, the significant point about al-Haytham's theory is that the structure of his arguments is 'consistently experimental or mathematical'.

It was in the field of optics that a concept of experiment clearly emerged as an identifiable method of procedure in empirical enquiry. . . . The concept of testing, already found in astronomy, here explicitly appears as a distinct concept of experimental proof and it is by manipulative experiments that Ibn al-Haytham seeks to establish such properties of light as rectilinear propagation, reflection and refraction.

Professor Sabra emphasises the point because Islamic science is still often portrayed as obsessed with theory to the exclusion of experiment. A classic example of how theoretical and empirical science could complement each other is furnished by the enormous Islamic contribution to medicine. The medical authorities on whom Ibn al-Haytham drew were primarily the Greeks, Hippocrates, Galen and Dioscurides. Their works had been translated by Hunayn Ibn Ishaq and his colleagues in Baghdad in the previous (ninth) century and along with some Indian and Persian borrowings from Jundishapur, formed the basis of Arabic medicine. But not all Islamic physicians were content to accept this basis without question. Al-Razi (born in 865, known in Europe as Rhazes), arguably the most eminent of these physicians, made a point of treating each patient as a test case. In the hospitals of Rayy (near Tehran) and Baghdad he urged his pupils to keep a record of their treatment and observations and to consult with one another; his seminal work on measles and smallpox relied heavily on clinical observations. Al-Razi also made an outstanding contribution as a chemist – in which his love of experimentation was given full rein – and staunchly defended its companion science of alchemy; but anything else relating to magic or astrology he condemned. His last work, posthumously assembled, was a monumental collection of notes and patients' case histories entitled the *Hawi* (*Liber Continens*). From the viewpoint of the historian of medicine, the central importance of the *Hawi* cannot be over-emphasised. It quickly became the standard reference work of Arabic medicine, and remained so for centuries. Even in fourteenth-century Spain, at the other end of the Arabic-speaking world, it was still a primary source for medical authors such as Ibn al-Khatib (d. 1374).

But the central medical document of medieval times, and the most famous of all Arabic medical works was the *Qanun*, or *Canon* of Ibn Sina (980-1037), known in Europe as

Avicenna. The *Canon* dominated Middle Eastern medicine between the eleventh and nineteenth century, and European medicine until the seventeenth century, making it one of the most influential books ever written. Like Al-Razi, Ibn Sina was a genius of bewildering attainments. He had learnt the entire Quran by the time he was seven, and was a licensed physician by seventeen. His writings on philosophy and mathematics are as voluminous and almost as important as the *Qanun*, which, with its emphasis on the theory, organisation and classification of medical knowledge, must bear some responsibility for the image of Islamic science as disdaining experiment. Not that this theoretical emphasis disqualified it as science. On the contrary, in the medieval world as in the ancient, in Europe as in the East, this was precisely what science was about. Since Galen, physicians were often philosophers. Medicine was based on theories which were to be arranged and revalued to produce more convincing and comprehensive explanations of health and disease in the human organism. Even when Al-Razi criticised Hippocrates it was on the grounds of dialectical inconsistency and ambiguity. Ibn Sina also came in for criticism, usually for being too verbose or too clever. And by Ibn Zuhr (d. 1162, and known in Europe as Avenzoar) he was indeed accused of being obsessed with theory at the expense of practical observation. Ibn Zuhr was a protégé of the Almoravid dynasty of Spain and Morocco; and in Andalusia a medical school developed which was probably the most advanced in terms of clinical practice. But here too, theory, as evidenced in the medical work of Ibn Rushd (d. 1198, Averroes), the *Kulliyat*, continued to be dominant.

Nevertheless, in its practical application medicine was both organised and beneficial. Pharmacies were graded according to the proficiency of the dispenser and their drugs were sold under doctor's prescription. The hospital as a recognisable institution with sexually segregated wards of patients, resident doctors, dispensaries and teaching arrangements is also an Islamic creation. During the tenth and eleventh centuries such *bimaristans* were set up, usually under princely patronage, throughout the empire, the prototype being the eleventh-century Adudi *bimaristan* in Baghdad. Here twenty-four resident physicians, each with his complement of pupils, registrars and pharmacists formed a sizeable staff ministering to the needs of patients and promoting health care amongst the general public.

There were drugstores in most cities, towns and urban centres of the medieval Middle East. It is very likely that only the upper classes consulted the physicians, and the poor must have relied heavily on advice from the druggists. Where there were no drugstores, people must still have been able to buy their drugs from itinerant pedlars. We possess some unique information on the supply of drugs for the hospital in Tabriz in the first part of the fourteenth century, in a collection of about fifty letters by the physician Rashid al-Din Fadl Allah. Letter no. 18 asked the addressee to supply a long list of medicinal oils: six different kinds of oil from Shiraz; three from Syria; and three from Hilla, Iraq. The oils included those of violet, jasmine, narcissus, rose, myrtle, orange blossom, absinthe, mastic, camomile, castor oil and the oil of scorpions. Another letter (no. 21), addressed to an agent in Asia Minor, requested large quantities (50-100 maunds) of six drugs: anise seeds, agaric, mastic, lavender, dodder and wormwood. Letter no.42 reported the appointment of a new director to reorganise the hospital 'with some regard to the welfare of patients and supply of necessary drugs and medicaments'. The supply of drugs clearly was not limited to what could be produced locally. Many of the medicines which were not native to the heartland of the Middle East were imported from the Far East, Europe, or Africa. Drugs – that is herbs, spices and chemicals – were a large part of the goods which the medieval merchants handled. Ever since the Quranic injunctions concerning ablutions and the prohibition of unclean food, a concern for public hygiene also figured prominently in the works of Islamic writers. It received comprehensive treatment in a book of Ibn Butlan (d. 1068) which emphasised the benefits of diet, fresh air, exercise and emotional tranquility, and which enjoyed a wide currency in medieval Europe.

Arab Muslim scholars made frequent attempts to classify the whole range of sciences known in their day, and to fit each one into a hierarchical whole. In most of these schemes of classification a distinction is drawn between the 'religious', or 'Islamic' science (Law, Quran and Hadith studies), and those known as 'ancient' or 'rational' sciences (the philosophical and natural sciences). With the literary arts (Arabic and grammar) as a distinct science, these three divisions were fundamental to both scholarship and education.

The master science of medieval Arabic civilisation was that of Islamic law, and it was this discipline which dominated the institutions of higher learning and formal education. From the eleventh century onward, the college of law, or *madrassah*, signified the dominance of Islamic law as the queen of the sciences. The curriculum of these colleges excluded the rational sciences, although there are instances of professors of law teaching medicine or philosophy (on the side, as it were). But the religious sciences could not be studied without Arabic, and grammar was therefore a formal part of the curriculum.

Medicine was less controversial than most of the other 'rational' sciences. Care of the body was in accordance with Islamic teaching and a medical knowledge of its functioning could only provide evidence of the wisdom of God. There was no conflict; rationalist thinkers, whose philosophy might be considered as heresy, could earn an honest living as medical practitioners. And although medicine never found a place in the syllabuses of the orthodox schools of mosque and *madrassah*, the fact that training was institutionalised in the hospitals is evidence of its acceptable status; most of the other sciences were taught only informally (and with no official patronage, after the eleventh century).

The debate over what was in conformity with Islamic teaching and what was not, raged during the Middle Ages in the other 'rational' sciences. For mathematics and astronomy the main problem was that the Greek legacy connected them with what became identified as astrology. By dabbling in astrology the philosopher/scientist had a chance of rich patrons, but this did not mean its acceptance by Islamic jurisprudence. 'The planets', according to al-Kindi, who had no qualms on the subject, 'are rational spiritual beings capable of intelligence and speech and who themselves cause and administer everything in this world by the order of the prime Creator who controls all.' In spite of the dutiful last phrase this was clearly a direct challenge to the fundamental Quranic doctrine of the unity of the Godhead.

Unlike al-Kindi, most scientific writers proceeded to disclaim astrological theories and none did so more vociferously or successfully than the mathematicians. Mathematics in fact became the one 'rational' or 'foreign' science to find a modest place in the curriculum of mosque and *madrassah*. Under this religious sanction it achieved great distinction, particularly in the synthesis of Greek and Indian methods of computation and of solving equations. The ninth-century *Kitab al-Jabr wa al-Muqabalah* of al-Khwarizmi established Arabic algebra (from al-Jabr), and his adoption of the Indian system of reckoning using nine fingers plus a zero gave Europe its so-called 'Arabic numerals'.

Astronomers were less successful in disassociating themselves from the taint of astrological prediction. Although the religious requirements for calendar computation and *qibla* orientation acted as a spur to observation and the construction of instruments, theoretical ideas about the universe remained those of Ptolemy, the main Greek influence. 'One is left with the impression that Islamic astronomers were engaged in correcting and re-correcting previous observations rather than testing newly imagined hypotheses', writes Professor Sabra. However, emphasis on the religious utility of astronomy eventually paid off with the establishment of the *muwaqqit*, a sort of religious time-keeper, in the twelfth century. This office, attached to the mosque, offered astronomers a new and respectable form of patronage. It also seems to have produced a belated but notable contribution to planetary theory, including a model for the superior planets developed by Ibn al-Shatir (d. 1375), *muwaqqit* of the Umayyad mosque in

Damascus, which may well have been appropriated by Copernicus.

Institutional patronage, and particularly the patronage of religious institutions, appears to have been a crucial element in the evolution of Islamic learning. Medicine, mathematics and astronomy all eventually found a roof within or beside the religious establishment. But astrology, alchemy and the occult sciences were excluded; and so too was philosophy. They were taught mostly in the private context of master and disciple, and their independence was ample compensation for the lack of institutionalism. As George Makdisi has recently written, 'The works in these fields which have come down to us are ample proof of their enthusiastic pursuit by scholars within the Muslim community.' The resultant profusion and prolixity of Arabic scholarship were truly remarkable. Since the twelfth century Europe has been indebted to it, yet only a fraction of its written output was translated in the Middle Ages and little more has been examined by modern scholarship. According to one estimate there are still a quarter of a million manuscripts in the libraries of the Muslim world and of the West. Many deal with scientific matters and many still await scrutiny.

* * *

In modern Kuwait – at KISR, in the hospitals and at the university – the relevance of medieval Islamic scholarship is epitomised in a revival of concern for the institutions and patronage of learning. In this atmosphere the exchange, synthesis and evaluation of ideas is stimulated. Kuwait may be on the periphery of the Arab world, but like tenth-century Baghdad, it attracts scholars and scientists from all the Arab countries and beyond. Dr Adnan Shihab al-Din, who now leads KISR, sees the medieval legacy as a source of both pride and encouragement.

What we are doing is not new. During the Arabic and Islamic civilisation we did exactly the same. Scientists from other civilisations came and worked in Baghdad, Alexandria and Damascus and they brought with them the scientific heritage from these other civilisations. When it was assimilated the new productivity of that new civilisation started. . . . The past tells me that there is a chance that we can do as well again. To that extent it motivates me as a challenge.

In a complex and rich sense, medieval science provides an inspiring example of scientific activity and originality to contemporary Arabs. The actual product of medieval science is something else again, of course. A line of poetry written a thousand years ago can still affect a modern Arab; there is no Arab who has been to school in the last fifty years who cannot recite by heart lines of the great tenth-century poet, Mutannabi:

> Not everything a man hopes he gets,
> Winds run against the course of ships.

But Ibn Sina's theory of humours to explain disease, for instance, cannot hope to have the same practical presence in the mind of modern Arabs, any more than the theories of Harvey or Newton have a contemporary relevance to British medicine or physics. What these men did belongs now to the international heritage of scientific history.

125

The work of a scientist in any country must, by its specialist nature, be remote from the great majority of people. But despite this, there is an important sense in which the folk-tradition of knowledge is perpetuated and, these days thanks to the media, made available to the masses. Ibn Sina may still be seen on television by many an Arab, diagnosing a love-sick youth by the rate of his pulse! Even such a simple example is not to be despised, since it adds to the sense of past achievement. For pride in the past is pride in a specific past. As Kuwaitis emphasise the medieval Arab-Islamic achievement, and since that achievement stems from a wide area – from Cairo, Damascus, Baghdad, and other places – it becomes clear that there is even more at stake than national pride. From Kuwait to Syria, from Egypt to Morocco, modern Arabs actively acquire the same points of historical and cultural reference, and a common sense of identity.

1. *Portrait of Aristotle with his pupil, Alexander the Great, from 'The Description of Animals' by Ibn Bakhtishū, early 13th century. Stories of Aristotle's tutorship of Alexander were popular and widely circulated in a civilisation whose breadth of conquests paralleled Alexander's*

Arab curiosity about the physical world, its origin and man's place in it, was fired by the legacy of Greek scholarship. The translation of works by – and commentaries on – Euclid, Galen, Hippocrates, Ptolemy, Plato and Aristotle was undertaken by scholars working under the Caliph's patronage in the ninth and tenth centuries. The extent to which these 'foreign' sciences, and especially Aristotelian metaphysics, were compatible with Quranic revelation was hotly debated for many centuries. But at the same time these texts seeded the evolution of scientific thought in what was the dominant culture of the period – medieval Islam.

2. (above) Water-wheels or 'norias' on the Orontes river in Hamat, Syria. Such wheels have been *i* use since the 12th century

3. (left) An irrigation canal in the Hasa oasis, Hofhof, Saudi Arabia

4. (right) A twin-cylinder pump from Al-Jazari's 'Book of Knowledge of Ingenious Mechanic* Devices' (1206)

Only a few examples of medieval Islamic technology survive. But in Al-Jazari *Book of Knowledge of Ingenious Mechanical Devices' (1206) a variety* elaborate water-clocks, pumps, musical automata and trick vessels are describ* and illustrated from the author's personal experience. Many, including *t* twin-cylinder pump (4) relied on water pressure. Others, using draught animals power water-hoists, were more sophisticated than many such devices still common in use in the Third World. The Arab engineer of today can thus look back on a lor* tradition of technological achievement, especially in irrigation works.

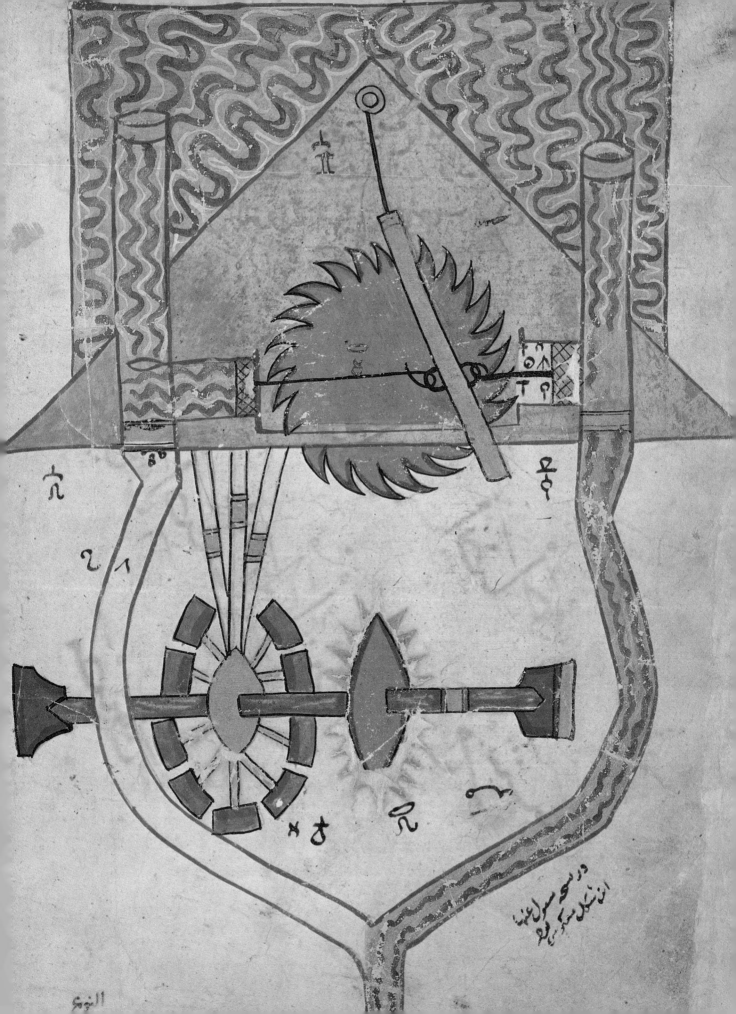

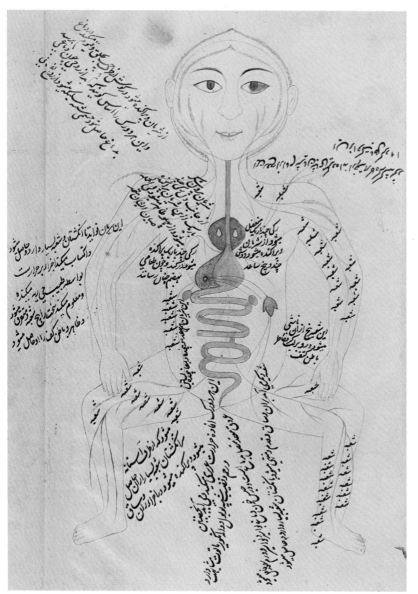

5. An anatomical plate illustrating the circulation of the blood, from a 17th-century Persian 'Medical Treasury'

6. From the 'Kitab al-Tasrif' of Abu' l' Qasim az-Zahrawi (d.1013). Written in Muslim Spain, this is probably the first encyclopaedic work of medical instruction and practice. This page includes illustration of various kinds of scalpels, scrapers, hooks and forceps, some of which were used in obstetric surgery

For 800 years the Islamic world led the way in medical science. Through the works of Avicenna (Ibn Sina) and others this knowledge was shared with the outside world; from it stemmed the medical advances made in Europe and America in the past two centuries. It embraced all aspects of prevention and treatment from public hygiene to surgery (6) and all aspects of theory and practice from anatomy (5) to pharmacy (7). As a recognisable institution with wards, resident doctors and a teaching programme, the hospital made its first appearance in eighth-century Baghdad and rapidly spread throughout the Islamic world.

7. From a 13th-century Baghdad manuscript, Istafan ibn Basil's translation of Dioscorides' treatise on herbs

8. *Reflecting dishes at a solar energy plant in Kuwait*

Like Archimedes, Ibn-al-Haytham (b.965) experimented with magnifying mirrors to concentrate light and heat and imagined their use in battle. The dishes at the solar power plant of the Kuwait Institute for Scientific Research (8) utilise a related technology. Al-Haytham also formulated an important new theory of vision combining mathematical and geometrical reasoning with physiological and physchological explanations of perception.

9. *An illustration of principles described in Ibn al-Haytham's 'Optics' written in Egypt in the early 11th century. It comes from a 14th-century Latin version of the 'Optics'*

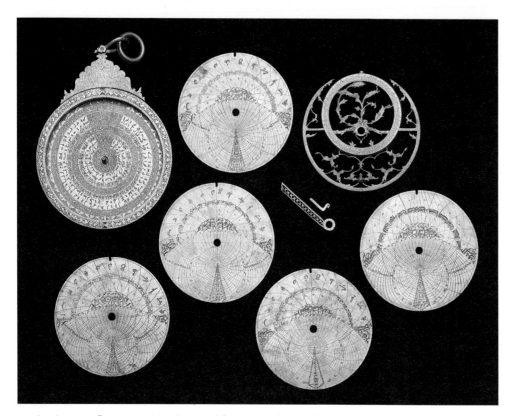

10. A 17th-century Persian astrolabe, dismantled. In itself a model of the Heavens, the astrolabe was used to measure angular distances beginning with the altitude of the sun or a star, and to solve, by the mechanical operation of its parts, difficult computations, the times of sunrise and sunset for example.   11. From Abd al-Rahman al Sufi's 'Figures of the Stars', 10th century, which rapidly became the most authoritative source on observational astronomy in the Islamic world

For calculating the correct orientation of prayer and the exact timing of Ramadan an understanding of planetary theory and instruments of astronomical observation were essential. Observatories, like that at Maragha, produced astronomical tables of great accuracy and the instruments which they developed, such as astrolabes (10) and quadrants, gave an early impetus to navigation.

That Arab science was prompted by a genuine curiosity about the natural world rather than just a love of knowledge for its own sake is well attested by the accounts of a succession of great travellers. Many of them – Ibn Battuta, Leo Africanus – came from the Maghreb, including Al-Idrisi, born in Morocco in 1100. After studying in Cordoba and wandering the length of the Arab world he settled in Sicily and there distilled his knowledge into a dish shaped map made of solid silver. The map, and the book on which it was based, show the application of scientific methods in formulating the shape of the earth and filling in its topography (12). Al-Idrisi is thus one of the pioneers of modern geography.

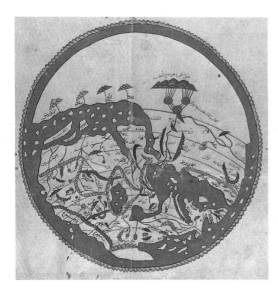

12. (left) Asia, Europe and North Africa from the great atlas of Al-Idrisi, 1154

13. (on facing page) In the observatory at Maragha, founded in 1259 by the Il-Khanid ruler Huleg the great scientist Nasir ad-Din at-Tusi is at work with his collaborators. The miniature is from manuscript of the Nusret-nama, Bukara, 16th century

CHAPTER SEVEN

WOMEN
AND THE
FAMILY

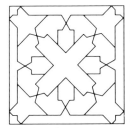Women constitute one half of society and, when it comes to generalisations, prove just as diverse, perverse and inscrutable as the other half. In some Arab countries, women in the cities may appear to enjoy greater freedom and equality than in the rural areas; in others, it is the other way round. Similarly, whereas women of high social rank led the emancipation struggle in Egypt, in Algeria emancipation is more evident amongst the lower classes. Education does not necessarily mean more independence; nor does the existence on the statute book of liberating legislation. That will depend very much on how the law is actually applied and how many women are aware of their rights and willing to test them.

Political change can be charted in official pronouncements and economic change can be measured in statistics; social change is altogether more elusive. Observers wishing to judge the state of society in unfamiliar cultures therefore have easy recourse to a political indicator which, in the case of Muslim countries, may often be the status of women. Their status has usually been judged in terms of legal standing – readily ascertainable – and whether or not they wear a veil – even easier to ascertain. But these simple criteria are wholly inadequate and not a little misleading. As for the veil, it has latterly proved to be as much a symbol of progressive as of retrogressive social trends, for both veiling and unveiling have signified liberation of a sort.

The first steps on the road to women's rights in the Arab world are generally traced back to the days in 1919 when there was a major Egyptian nationalist movement against the British. Huda Sharawi took part alongside her husband, an important figure in the movement, and she went on to lead women in demonstrations against the British, becoming widely respected and admired. One day, returning from a women's conference in Rome in 1923, she took off the veil before a startled welcoming committee on the quay at Alexandria. She and her sister feminists remained unveiled, and that movement spread too. From the 1920s until the 1970s the use of the veil steadily declined until now only a minority of Arab women outside the conservative societies of the Arabian Peninsula still use it. When the girls on the sewing machines at Abdelmalek Tazi's leather factory in Fez clock off, some put on a veil, others do not. Even the veiled ones can hardly be considered rigid conservatives if they have worked all day veil-less on an unsegregated shop floor. In Morocco, as in most other Arab countries, the veil is neither legally obligatory nor prohibited. But why, the Westerner might reasonably ask, should women be *made* to veil or unveil? Why cannot Muslim women choose for themselves?

They do. Many young women in Egypt, Jordan, Tunisia and elsewhere have, in the last few years, returned to traditional Muslim dress. (The term 'veil' may mislead; the traditional Islamic dress code which the young girls invariably adopt covers the hair and neck, but the face itself remains uncovered.) These girls are often the daughters of mothers who were unveiled and the granddaughters of women like Huda Sharawi who threw off the veil in the 1920s as a sign of liberation. For these granddaughters of the 1980s, its *adoption* is a sign of protest – protest against Western influence in its new and perhaps more insidious form. By taking on Muslim dress they return to an indigenous culture and symbolise their liberation from a foreign culture which has been imposed on them.

We became Muslims not to follow previous values, but to follow our own new values. And we are not forcing anybody to follow our values – we will not take our own values and impose them on Christians, on Western life . . . What I say right, they will say wrong. I say that this dress is to protect my dignity as a woman; Simone de Beauvoir will say that it is an attack against women and a violation of her dignity. I will not go and force Simone de Beauvoir to put on Muslim dress. And I refuse Simone de Beauvoir to go to Imam Khomeini to tell him with rudeness 'Don't apply this Muslim rule on Muslim women.' By God, this is very strange.

Safinaz Kazim, an Egyptian journalist and drama critic, is one of a number of eloquent women – university students and graduates, doctors and lawyers – who have chosen to wear traditional Islamic dress. But again the important point about the veil in the twentieth century is that it has been subject to a variety of interpretations. Cultural and political definitions are modified by the individual:

I took up Muslim dress a year and a half ago because this is part of Islam and I believe in it. It is not one of the basic things in Islam, but it is just a framework. I feel I am pleasing God in this way. I feel that I should be a complete Muslim – not only obeying some of its rules and rejecting other rules.

These are the words of a young Egyptian medical student. Neither her status as a medical student nor her choice to veil are unusual and this fact illustrates the dilemma: is a young Egyptian woman attending medical school 'traditional' or 'modern'? Is training to be a doctor a 'liberating' or 'repressive' activity? And how does her free choice to wear Islamic dress qualify one's response to these questions?

For Arab women there are currently many important questions at hand: education, work and the challenge of combining career and family. The ideals of women's liberation as they have developed in the West are, to Arab men and women, often linked to the 'fragmentation' of Western society into the nuclear family. As Nadia Hijab, a Palestinian journalist who is editor of *The Middle East* magazine in London, explained, the extended family as a social support system is seen in the Arab world as superior to anything the welfare state has devised. The latter cares manfully for the bodily needs of its dependants – shelter, meals, benefits – but at the price of their psychological needs – respect, acceptance, affection. The family, as understood in the East, caters for both.

For us, the extended family not only provides warmth and love, it also functions as a social security system. It makes sure that orphans and widows are looked after within the family, and takes care of the ill and unemployed. And as for the elderly, to most Arabs it is unthinkable that their parents should end up in an old people's home. The warmth of a Middle Eastern family envelops you like a heavy cloak on a freezing day. Though I and many others might feel like casting that cloak off for a while when the sun is shining, I would never want to see it packed away for good.

Even after an arranged marriage to her cousin at the age of twelve, Om Gassem would agree. A Jordanian woman of about forty-five, Om Gassem lives in Amman. She is the first to admit that at the time her consent to her marriage was little more than a formality – 'I didn't have the sort of awareness to know what marriage meant. Yes, I accepted him and that was that.' But thirty-three years and ten children later, she knows, and she likes what she knows; for her it has worked well.

Two of her daughters are married and have moved out of the house, but the eldest son, who is also married, lives with his wife and two children in an annexe specially built on to the family home. His name is Gassem. Om Gassem simply means 'the mother of Gassem'. In the West, a woman changes her name on marriage. In most Arab countries women keep their maiden name, but an important change of first name for both man and woman comes with the birth of the first son, an indication of the importance of children (especially boys, the future breadwinners) in Arab society.

To all appearances the family of Om Gassem and her husband is typical. Early betrothal and marriage to a cousin are still common; the former is seen as an effective way of obviating the risk of pre-marital sexual encounters and the latter as a way of cementing broader family ties and of ensuring social compatibility. In a society where marriage is a social contract rather than a romantic proposition, the wedding must be arranged, and financial agreements are written into the contract. If the extended family is to work as a social institution, its central linkage is far too crucial to be left to the whims of teenage attachments; as Om Gassem sees it – 'These days the girl goes her own way and

138

then in a couple of years you'll find that they're getting divorced. The proper way is for them to accept the advice of their elders.'

For one of Om Gassem's generation, the fact that she received no formal education is unremarkable. In the 1940s there were few schools and fewer parents who considered female education essential. It is also unremarkable that, even as a child, Om Gassem rebelled against social constraints and sought education. Pretending she was going to call on her aunt, she used to sneak out of the house and attend the only school for girls – a Christian school – in her village. One day, 'My mother went and asked my aunt if I was there, and she said she hadn't seen me in days. When I went home, my mother gave me a really good hiding. So I repented and that was the end of my schooldays.' Om Gassem has since joined an adult literacy class and learned the rudiments of reading and writing. Her deprivation made her determined – as it did mothers all over the Arab world – that her daughters would receive an education. Three have now completed their high school education, and go out to work.

The number of girls in school throughout the Arab world has by now caught up with the number of boys, and they are fast catching up at the university level. With the rising cost of living – described as a 'liberating force' for women by one Arab labour expert – more and more women are going out to work. In 1960 less than 2% of Jordan's women were earning an income (women working in farming are still not officially considered 'workers' in the region and their figures rarely show on the statistics). By 1983, the number of women working in Jordan had risen to 17%; the government, as in many Arab countries, has a deliberate policy to encourage women to work. Jordan has lost much of its skilled manpower to better paying jobs in the Gulf (some 305,000 people), and actually imports labour. It is thus investing a good deal of money to 'broaden the base of the employment market by turning every available Jordanian into a skilled worker', as the labour minister put it, to the tune of some JD45 million (about £90 million) in training women alone.

The effect of inflation and the need for the family to earn an extra income was neatly summed up by Rami Khouri, former editor of the *Jordan Times*. He pointed out:

In the last three years when you had higher inflation in Jordan than we ever had, families realised that the wife or daughter who graduated from high school or college could bring in an extra 100 dinars or so a month. If a woman could move into a job – say in a factory, a school or a hospital – that was not violently against social tradition, then the social obstacles melted away, like a knife cutting through butter.

Apart from enacting the labour laws necessary to enable women to work, Jordan has instituted a Ministry of Social Development, headed by Mrs Inaam Mufti, one of whose major aims is to integrate women into development. Khouri went so far as to say:

I think the question of women in the workforce is going to become very important in the late 1980s. After two or three more years of putting the social and industrial infrastructure into place, the Arab world is going to realise that half of its most valuable resource is unutilised.

Om Gassem, an enterprising lady, waited for no man. Twenty years ago she and her husband had moved to the city from her home village in the north, so that her husband could take up a job as a carpenter at a government department. Once the rising cost of living began to cut into her husband's earnings, she went to work – but again surreptitiously, as she had attempted to study as a child. By now she has developed a thriving business in antiques and crafts, buying goods from the countryside and selling them in the city: 'I did my buying and selling while he was working. As soon as he left the house, I used to go and get the things and go to the museum in Amman and sell them. Before he got back, the food was ready and everything was as it should be.' When her husband found out, he was furious. What would people say if they knew he had come to rely on his wife's help to provide for his children; in his family, women did not go out to work. But economic necessity is a powerful persuader, as Om Gassem explained: 'You know life is expensive and one needs more money – people should help each other. I am not educated, I can't go and teach somewhere. This business is a clean and honest job. So in the end he joined me and we went to the villages together, and now it's a family business.'

Arab women have not only moved out of the house and into the workplace, they have also moved beyond such 'traditionally' acceptable jobs as teaching, nursing and secretarial. Indeed, they have entered almost every field in the Arab world: there are women government ministers, doctors, lawyers, judges, engineers, designers, business executives, publishers. In Amman, the national carrier Alia boasts two female airline pilots, one of them the first woman in the world to pilot a Tristar. But whereas working women have increased in number, facilities to enable them to cope with both career and family have lagged behind. And there are, needless to say, strong conservative currents that seek to pull women back into the traditional role of wife and mother to the exclusion of all else. Still, as Nadia Hijab put it, 'The Arab world is a surprisingly pragmatic place. If you have skill and determination you earn respect and the right to pursue your own path.'

The early Egyptian feminists of the first half of the twentieth century, led by Huda Sharawi, went on to lobby for women's right to education, the right to vote and equal rights in other fields, establishing a number of centres for women on the way. But for today's feminists in Egypt, the early feminists did not go nearly far enough. As doctor and writer Nawal el Sadawi put it:

They wanted to educate girls in schools and universities and they wanted to change the law. But what was their philosophy? Why did they do this? They were very short-sighted. They thought that a woman could not live without a husband. And if she acquired education, she did so in order to help her husband and to help the family, not to help herself as a person.

Nawal el Sadawi believes it is now time to take women's emancipation a step further, and calls for the foundation of a feminist union that would be a powerful political movement. She feels that the sporadic economic crises that have pushed women into the workforce have not changed their overall position. The problem is, as ever in both the Arab world and the rest of the world, what to do with the family.

Whenever we say we want to liberate women, they say 'But what about the family, who's going to take care of the children and the husband?' But women have been exploited for years because of that family, because it is a patriarchal family. What I say is that we do not want to destroy the family but we want to destroy the patriarchal family – a type of family in which the husband is the authority, the absolute authority. He owns the children, he owns the wives. That's what we have to change.

And how does one change it? According to Dr Sadawi, the first thing is to understand the origin and sanction of the patriarchal family. She, like most Muslim reformers, draws a firm distinction between what religion in the form of Revelation has to say about it and what religion in the form of Islamic law has made of it. Most authorities agree that the Quran and the teachings of the Prophet were intended to improve the status of women in Arabian society. This is particularly evident in such general ethical recommendations as, for instance, that women must be respected and wives treated fairly and not divorced without good reason. It is also evident in the Quran's more specific legal pronouncements, but only if these are seen against the background of existing, pre-Islamic, practice.

To take the best-known example – the Quran says that a man can have up to four wives. In the seventh century, in Arabia as in other parts of the world, there were no doubt sound social and economic reasons for polygamy. Outside of the family a woman had no status and it was therefore meritorious to marry widows of whom, in turbulent times, there were many. Marriage was also a guarantee of political and commercial alliances and of intra-tribal solidarity. As so often was the case, Islam had the effect of legalising existing practice but also modifying and humanising it. If, as was indeed the case, seventh-century society had placed no restrictions on the number of wives the Quranic sanction of just four can be seen as an attempt to restrict polygamy. That it was also meant to protect the rights of wives in a polygamous marriage becomes clear from the provision that the husband must treat each of them equally. A hadith of the Prophet relates the dilemma of a husband trying to follow this precept to the letter. He is dividing a bunch of grapes between his two wives but unfortunately the bunch is of an uneven number. Instead of eating the last one himself he cannot resist giving it to her whom at heart he loves best. Such human frailty could be taken to mean that no man can display the impartiality necessary to qualify for more than one wife. This is the construction put upon it by many modernist scholars and on it rests the legal prohibition of polygamy which, of all the Arab countries, so far only Tunisia has adopted. But even without legal prohibitions polygamy is naturally dying out in the modern world, and this is as much a response to the economic and social pressures of today as, once, was polygamy.

Feminist reformers like Nawal Sadawi argue that Islamic law itself must adapt to modern times. If Islamic law was based on practice as they contend, then it should take account of contemporary practice which has already responded to social and economic change. The assumption is, of course, that laws regarding women would thus become more liberal or progressive. But the reinterpretation of Islamic law to suit modern conditions is not without unexpected ironies: in the important case of legislation concerning birth control in the Islamic world, modern social trends have persuaded many jurists to reverse or suppress a remarkably liberal tradition.

All the Islamic schools of law from the tenth to the nineteenth century gave contraception their serious consideration. The Muslim jurists dealt principally with *coitus interruptus*, historically the most common method, and unanimously agreed that *coitus interruptus* was licit provided the wife gave her permission. The jurists based their permission on the free woman's consent because she had rights to children and complete sexual fulfilment which withdrawal was judged to diminish. From the writings of the jurists it emerges that other methods of birth control – mostly intravaginal tampons – were used by women and the commonest view was that these should only be employed if the husband also agreed.

Given the date and the fact that both Jewish and Christian tradition outlawed contraception, the interesting conclusion must be that Muslims had a remarkably pragmatic and sophisticated attitude towards family planning and a wide and intelligent knowledge of possible methods. Medieval Arabic medical writers devoted special chapters to contraception and abortion, always paying attention to birth control as a normal part of the physician's art. The explanations given by medieval Muslims for why one might choose to practise birth control were as often personal as economic, social or medical. According to them, birth control was used to avoid the material hardships of a large number of dependants; to safeguard property; to guarantee the education of a child; to protect a woman from the dangers of childbirth, especially if she was young or sickly; or simply to preserve her health and beauty.

In modern times, Catholics who wish to modify church teachings on contraception have difficulty in locating a basis for permission in the Catholic tradition. Ironically, the modern Muslims who face similar difficulties are those who wish to prohibit birth control. The irony is compounded by the fact that both pro-birth control Catholics and anti-birth control Muslims are reacting to new modern conditions.

During the four decades following the Second World War 'over-population', particularly in the Third World, has engaged the efforts of national governments, international agencies, but also foreign Western institutions and governments. Responding both to government involvement in their personal lives, and to the jealous advocacy of family planning by some Western circles, a number of Muslims have seen the whole effort as another foreign intervention to manipulate the destiny of Muslim communities.

When birth control was introduced again as a question in twentieth-century Islam it produced a normal response – the Muslim jurist consulted his old books and repeated the classical permission. The reaffirmation of the classical permission remained the more typical reaction of modern jurists even after population control became a controversial question from the 1950s on. The jurist answered affirmatively when he was asked a narrow question: Is contraception licit in Islam?

But Islamic law had never envisioned birth control as a concern of the state. The Islamic religious permission applied to individual couples, who alone had the right to limit their families according to their own economic, medical or personal interest. And gradually, as between 1952 and 1975 over three-quarters of all Muslims came to live under governments with official family planning programmes, fears and resentment of their implications have persuaded a number of religious leaders to confront the classical permission and forthrightly to reject it. Sadly both this stance and the population policies it attacks are equally distant from the spirit of classical Islamic law and its view of birth control as strictly a matter of personal choice.

* * *

Without their own engagement in the process of interpreting and enacting Islamic law, women will remain vulnerable to its currents. Badria al-Awadi, who became the first

woman to head the Faculty of Law and Islamic Sharia (Islamic law) at Kuwait
University, explained:

Our first problem as women in the Arab or Muslim world is that we don't know our legal rights. And that's
very dangerous. If you don't know your rights you can't protect yourself. The reason behind it is that
women have not been participating in the process of interpreting Islamic law or enacting civil legislation.

More women are involved in this field today. In Tunisia, which boasts one of the most
progressive family laws in the Arab world and which provides equal rights for women in
terms of divorce and custody of the children, women are often represented by women
lawyers, and women judges sit in the courts. The latest amendments to the family code
give women an even stronger position on alimony and housing in cases of contested
divorce – so much so that men have begun to protest, and some women blame the law for
a drop in the number of marriage proposals.

Tunisia is not alone in the region in being caught in the difficult transition between
tradition and modernity. Working women (and men) are expected to continue to live
with their families until they set up their own family. It is very rarely that an individual
sets up his or her own establishment. This has led to cases like that of Zohra, a
twenty-six-year-old Tunisian nutritionist, who finds that she is treated exactly like her
male colleagues at work, earning the same salary, but hemmed in by tradition at home.
She lives with her uncle's family, her parents having divorced when she was a child, and
finds it difficult to cope.

I love my uncle's family but for some years our relationship has been strained. They don't let me do
anything but my work. They don't let me learn how to drive. I've taken up sport and dancing, and when
they found out they tried to stop me, but I continue in secret.

The freedom we girls want is the freedom to do what we want. After all we are adults; our parents are not
going to guide us at our age. They are now beginning to recognise the fact that I come home late in the
evenings. At one point they told me to leave the house. I told them fine, that suits me. So I started to look
for an apartment. Unfortunately I had to give up. Living with them is like living alone. We don't think alike
politically or socially. We are not the same generation and they should recognise this.

Zohra may partly solve her problem by, as she intends, going abroad to continue her
studies. But it will not be completely solved until both generations adapt to the
differences in each other and to the changing world around them.

An Arab girl is generally more restricted than a boy because her fate is inextricably tied
to the concept of family honour. In many parts of the Arab world a woman will not go out
unless chaperoned by a male relative. The strict moral code is not, of course, a peculiarly
Arab idea; it was the same in Victorian England, and it has been relaxed in the
cosmopolitan areas of the Arab world today. But the underlying tensions caused by the

code are still there. As Nawal el Sadawi explained:

This is an area that is really very sensitive; up till now the conception of honour is related to the sexual morality, virginity and fidelity of the female sex only. And this conception of honour puts a lot of restriction to the movement – and to the intellectual freedom – of the woman. In the name of honour girls are kept in the house to be married very early; an intelligent wife may be kept in the house by her husband.

Crimes of honour – where a male relative may kill his sister or daughter if she is even suspected of misdoing – are still treated leniently by the courts.

For Arab women, the difficulties exist and the opportunities exist. Progress will be slow because neither women nor society want to tear away at the most sacred of Arab institutions, the family. If, for example, Om Gassem's daughters feel a little hampered by their relative lack of freedom (they enjoy more freedom than Zohra) they will joke about it, argue, voice irritation and try to cajole their parents into a compromise. Om Gassem's sons will alternately take their sisters' side or demand even more modest behaviour of them. Two of the grown-up sons envisage allowing their wives to work if they want to when they get married; a third wouldn't dream of it and would keep her at home to look after him and his children. With the exception of one daughter, who is afraid she will find more restrictions on her movements by a future husband than by her father's family, all of Om Gassem's children think in terms of family – their own, their parents. As one daughter put it, 'Even though I am married and I live in my own house, I still miss the days when I was living with my family. The little quarrels, the arguments over who will watch which television programme or who will sleep where, even these little things are dear to us.' Om Gassem summed it up for all her family: 'We cannot do without each other.'

2. *A Moroccan fami...*

3. *Nawal el Sadawi*

'Whenever we say we want to liberate women, they say "But what about the family, who's going to take care of the children and husbands?" Women have been exploited for years because of that family. What I say is that we do not want to destroy the family but we want to destroy the patriarchal family – a type of family in which the husband is the absolute authority . . . That's what we have to change.' Nawal el Sadawi (3) is an outspoken Egyptian feminist who believes that the family can survive without the traditional dominance of its menfolk. Others, seeing the loosening of family ties in the West, are less sure. But all concede that whilst equal rights and opportunities may be desirable for both sexes, the family must come first.

'The warmth of a Middle Eastern family envelops you like a heavy cloak on a freezing day. Though I and many others might feel like casti...
that cloak off for a while when the sun is shining, I would never want to see it packed away for good.' – Nadia Hejab

Facing page: 4. (top left) Zabid in the Yemen Arab Republic 5. (top right) Dubai, United Arab Emirates 6. (bottom) A Berber family in the village of Imlil in Moroc...

7. (above) A woman leads a train of donkeys and camels across the Aures mountains of Algeria

8. (below) Corn harvesting in the village of Imlil, Morocco

9. (facing page) A fruitseller in Egypt

Except among the higher classes, Arab women have always worked outside the home and have often exercised a real authority commensurate with the respect that is their traditional due.

10. *(facing page) Dar el-Hanan Girls school in Jeddah, Saudi Arabia*

11. *(above) Police cadets in Aman*

12. *(below) Television factory, Algeria*

Female education, though often segregated, is now the rule rather than the exception. The teachings of the Prophet are widely acknowledged as having been intended to initiate a process of female emancipation. In recent times this process has been reactivated by the involvement of women in the nationalist struggle and the espousal of socialist policies. As teachers, health workers, and even lawyers, women themselves have been promoting female advancement. Today, increasingly, they are adopting less obvious professions in industry, communications, and services.

CHAPTER EIGHT

THE
SHADOW OF
THE WEST

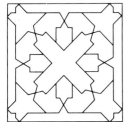

It was one evening. I was going home from the Gezira Club; my father was a member. We lived nearby and I was just walking across the grass and going to go through the fence to our house. There was a sort of bicycle track there and I saw this helmeted figure approaching along it. I remember his name; he was called Pelly, fresh-faced, pith-helmet, you know. He said, 'What are you doing here?' I said, 'I'm just going home. I've come from the Club. I'm going home.' He said, 'But you're an *Arab*; you shouldn't be here.'

For Edward Said, Professor of English and Comparative Literature at New York's Columbia University, the realisation that he was *different* came some thirty-five years ago when he was a schoolboy in Cairo. Now a popular and expansive intellectual, he exudes the urbanity of the Ivy Leaguer; if being an Arab in the USA is to be somehow handicapped he has convincingly 'overcome' it. But the American academic is not just any Arab; he is a Palestinian. And Professor Said resents bitterly the ideas inherent in the notion that his nationality should constitute a handicap or that the conjunction of his two identities should be considered in any way improbable.

When I started to be concerned about the Middle East and to write about it a new component was added to my social identity. As a Professor of Literature I became also a Palestinian activist. It has its own rewards because you are not constrained by just being a specialist; you live in a different world. But otherwise I have found it a very heavy burden to bear, not only because of what people say – you acquire enemies and so on – but also because frankly, I spend a great deal of my time being angry. You're constantly aware, you know, not so much of the direct pressure but I mean wherever you turn . . . you read a bit of the newspaper or see it on television and wherever you turn we're never described in terms that don't offend. I mean you can't simply be reduced to a person who just throws bombs. And worse still, nobody ever tries to understand, if you were to throw a bomb, why you might be doing it. It's assumed you're doing it because historically that's the way Arabs are. They're just killers and bomb throwers.

Being an Arab in British Egypt meant being 'not supposed to be there' and being a Palestinian in New York means being a 'bomb thrower'. Amongst the large Arab community in Detroit this discriminatory phenomenon is taken for granted. 'They think we all hitch-hiked [hi-jacked] a plane to get here.' 'They call us CJ's – that stands for 'camel-jockeys'. First camel I saw was in the zoo here.' Admittedly national stereotypes are rarely flattering. But Professor Said's anger stems from the belief that, in the case of the Arabs, the West has never explored beyond such standardised preconceptions. And that European and American policy towards the Arab world has actually been dictated, and is actually dictated, by these jaundiced preconceptions.

In 1978 Said threw down his gauntlet to the West in the publication of *Orientalism*. His technique was incisive – examining the relationship between, on the one hand, Western notions of the Arab Middle East as expressed and implied in the writings of the French and British orientalists and, on the other, the historical events and political attitudes which they informed. Said wreaks havoc among the orientalists – travellers, scholars, creative writers and statesmen – not just for *mis*-representing the East, but for the way they represented it. That is, 'the fact that the orientalist, poet or scholar, makes the Orient speak, describes the Orient, renders its mysteries plain, for and to the West.'

He is never concerned with the Orient except as the first cause of what he says. What he says and writes, by virtue of the fact that it is said and written, is meant to indicate that the Orientalist is outside the Orient, both as an existential and as a moral fact. . . .

A characteristic of orientalist representation of the East is the isolation of a single insight or impression and its adoption as 'significant' of a pan-oriental trait. 'An observation about a tenth-century Arab poet multiplied itself into a policy towards (and about) the oriental mentality in Egypt, Iraq or Arabia. Similarly a verse from the Quran would be considered the best evidence of an ineradicable Muslim sensuality.' This selective approach is as revealing about the orientalists and their own culture as about the East. Professor Said believes that a culture defines itself by contrast with some alien and fanciful entity. Traditionally the Orient, portrayed as a land of mystery and luxury, of cruelty and anarchy, of ignorance, venality, depravity and superstition, was used to boost Europe's self-image as a bastion of morality, order and enlightenment. Orientalism became a 'vision of reality whose structure promoted the difference between the familiar (Europe, the West, 'us') and the strange (the Orient, the East, 'them').'

This vision in a sense created and then served the two worlds thus conceived. Orientals lived in their world, 'we' in ours. The vision and material reality propped each other up, kept each other going.

This oriental 'otherness' was both fearful (the ruthless Saracen, the Islamic fundamentalist) and titillating (the harem, the gold cadillac). Today, with expanding horizons, we have another, galactic, arena of 'otherness'; science fiction provides an instructive parallel of the function once discharged by the more fanciful purveyors of orientalism.

But according to Said, the orientalists' 'vision of reality' was not primarily cultural; it was political. The attempt to acquire knowledge about a people in order to represent them to others assumes an intellectual superiority and mastery over them. And if it worked in the realm of ideas it could work in the realm of politics. Orientalism thus became imperialism and the works of the orientalist inspired and legitimised the work of the empire-builder. For this part of his argument Said increasingly narrows down the Orient to Egypt and the eastern Arab world. Many might fault his indictment of orientalism as it was understood in, say, India (which for the British was more typically the Orient but which Said largely ignores); others might even question his selection of Middle Eastern orientalists (what, for instance, of W. S. Blunt who not only condemned British rule in Egypt but also supported Arab nationalism?). But as Said advances and concentrates his argument still further he shows how orientalist attitudes, though changed to the extent that the West's view of 'otherness' changed, continued to inform the perfidy of the Sykes-Picot agreement, the conceit of the Balfour Declaration, the tragedy of Palestine, and the injustice of US policy today. Here the force and fury of his statement carries all before it.

When Orientals struggle against colonial occupation you must say that Orientals have never understood the meaning of self-government the way 'we' do. . . . Or you say that if Arab Palestinians oppose Israeli settlement and occupation of their lands, then that is merely 'the return of Islam', or as a renowned contemporary orientalist defines it, Islamic opposition to non-Islamic peoples, a principle of Islam enshrined in the seventh century. History, politics and economics do not matter. Islam is Islam, the Orient is the Orient, and please take all your ideas about a left and right wing, revolutions and change, back to Disneyland. For like its putative subject matter, Orientalism has not allowed ideas to violate its profound serenity. These contemporary Orientalist attitudes flood the press and the popular mind. Arabs, for example, are thought of as camel-riding, terroristic, hook-nosed, venal lechers whose undeserved wealth is an affront to real civilisation. Always there lurks the assumption that although the Western consumer belongs to a numerical minority, he is entitled to own or expend (or both) the majority of the world's resources. Why? Because he, unlike the Oriental, is a true human being.

But why did Professor Said, the American academic, the great authority on Joseph Conrad, become a Palestinian activist? Said was born in Jerusalem and in this hallowed but ambivalent city he sees the beginnings of an explanation. Jerusalem was, and is once again, the arena of East-West confrontation. In the Middle Ages map-makers actually showed it as being at the dead centre of the world, a third pole. But then as now the question was: Whose world? Whose pole? Whose city? For Jews it is the Western (Wailing) Wall and the Temple Mount; for Christians it is Calvary and the Church of the Holy Sepulchre; and for the Muslims it is the Dome of the Rock and the al-Aqsa Mosque. Each of the monotheistic religions has a claim on the place which dispossession never dims. Psalm CXXXVII has done duty for Jew and Christian, and now for Muslim.

> If I forget thee, O Jerusalem, let my right hand forget her cunning.
> If I do not remember thee let my tongue cleave to the roof of my mouth;
> yea if I prefer not Jerusalem in my mirth.

The city is also the ancient capital of a culturally and strategically vital strip of land between the desert and the Mediterranean. But is this Palestine or Israel, the Holy Land or the Promised Land, Zion or Filastin? And what of the people who actually live there? For 1300 years Arabs, Jews, Muslims and Christians have farmed the 'land of milk and honey' and traded in 'Jerusalem the Golden'. Like Edward Said's family, they thought of the place as theirs by virtue of their living there. And indeed it was theirs, the flux of conquest and the demise of dynasties usually disturbing them little more than the flow of pilgrims.

Today all that has changed. The Palestinian people are dispersed or dispossessed and Jews, originally from the European metropoli, have replaced them. But the pilgrims and the tourists still come. They tour the sights in air-conditioned buses and walk the Via Dolorosa with well-conditioned minds. The fervour of faith and the cushioning of comfort inure them to the harsh realities of an occupied city. They seek not challenge but affirmation; and they find it. Like all previous visitors from the West they have expectations and preconceptions to which the city, the country and the East in general must conform.

First of their predecessors were the Crusaders. In 1096 when the first Crusade set out, Western Europe had only the haziest notion of the Orient. But its peoples, 'Moors' and 'Saracens', were familiar enough. For four hundred years Spain had been part of the Arab Islamic empire, a flourishing, opulent and civilised oasis during Europe's Dark Ages. At one point the Moorish armies had reached the Loire and, in Edward Gibbon's celebrated passage, were half way to the Scottish Highlands or the Polish frontier. But for Charles Martel's victory, 'the Arabian fleet might have sailed without a naval combat into the mouth of the Thames. Perhaps the interpretation of the Quran would now be taught in the schools of Oxford, and her pulpits might demonstrate to a circumcised people the sanctity and truth of the revelation of Mahomet.' Given the superiority of Islamic culture at the time this might have been no bad thing.

But by the late eleventh century the Christian powers were back on the offensive. Sicily had been retaken by the Normans and the reconquest of Spain was underway. When disturbances in the East interrupted Christian access to the Holy Places it seemed a logical step to take the fight to the enemy, to 'enter upon the road to the Holy Sepulchre, wrest it from a wicked race, and subject it to Christendom' in the words of Pope Urban. Already the Saracens represented a sense of Europe's otherness. They were feared as the blood-thirstiest of warriors, envied for their luxury and wealth but, above all, abhorred for the presumption of their religion. It was the idea that the Prophet superseded Christ which most rankled. He was 'the imposter' and his 'infidel' followers practised a 'superstition' that was uniquely detestable being both heathenism and heresy.

With heads filled with the grotesque misrepresentations of Islam put about by Christian polemicists, the Crusaders descended on the Levant. By fire and the sword – all graphically described in the Muslim chronicles of the period – the semi-barbarous invaders got their way; Palestine and Lebanon were carved up into Christian duchies and fiefdoms. A century later Salah-al-Din (Saladin) drastically reduced the Christian position and within a further century the Crusaders' last outposts were recaptured. Palestinians today are mindful of these events. The Crusades had few immediate repercussions but they established some important precedents. In Muslim eyes the Christians now appeared treacherous and bloodthirsty while in Christian eyes the Muslims were credited with a certain sophistication (usually characterised as 'decadence') and a certain nobility (in particular, chivalry). These two notions, the decadence and the nobility of the Arabs, took their place in the gallery of Oriental stereotypes alongside the 'wicked infidel'. More important, Europe had established a precedent, lastingly embodied in the great Crusader castles, for interfering and ordering the affairs of the Arab world and of Palestine in particular. The Holy Land had become a place of legitimate concern, almost an outpost of Europe, for which the Christian powers felt a unique responsibility.

But even symbols can be equivocal. In the summer of 1982 Beaufort Castle, or Ash-Shakif, was still in Arab hands – just. Gazing east to the Golan Heights and south to his forbidden homeland a Palestinian fighter saw a different significance in the story of the Crusades.

Saladin occupied this fortress, rebuilt it and added to it. From that time the fortress was known as Saladin's fortress because the Beaufort fortress was ruined when Saladin wanted to liberate the Arab land. Besides it was built on Arab land in the first place. Of course when Saladin liberated the fortress he used it as a point for preliminary mobilisation of forces in the direction of Palestine. From Ash-Shakif fortress the Arab and Islamic armies started their movement towards Palestine to liberate it from the Crusaders and the Christian colonialists who had come to our country in order to dominate the natural resources of the Orient.

The Crusades had failed, but through the Levantine trade of the Venetians and

Genoese, and through pilgrimage and travel, Western Europe preserved its links with the Eastern Mediterranean. Chaucer's knight, who had 'wonne Alisaundre', would not be returning for six hundred years but the Wife of Bath who 'thryes hadde . . . been at Jerusalem' was but the first in a long line of indomitable travellers. Their narratives, often informed by *The Thousand and One Nights* and significantly augmented by Galland's translation of that work in 1704, furnished Europe with a rich *pot-pourri* of images from which to select the most alien and arresting for inclusion in the gallery. To decadence were added indolence and sensuality; 'the gross clasp of a lascivious Moor' was an appropriate characterisation for Shakespeare's audience and three centuries later was even more recognisable and exciting for Delacroix's. As Europe forged ahead in the post-Renaissance period, the East became increasingly 'changeless', still 'decadent' but now sunk in age-old ignorance rather than sophistication. The nobility of the chivalrous Saladin was now transferred to the rude Bedouin, the 'noble savage' rather than the noble seigneur. Only Islam, or rather the pejorative 'Mohammedanism', remained an invariable component of Christian Europe's sense of oriental 'otherness'; without it there would have been no definition of Christian Europe. In Dante's Inferno the Prophet is accorded select treatment, being relegated to the eighth of Hell's nine gradations of iniquity (the ninth is reserved for the likes of Judas) and condemned to a particularly revolting, detailed and, of course, eternal process of evisceration.

The event which, in Professor Said's view, established that the orientalists' stereotypes were to be translated into a political reality (and, for Said, into a personal reality) was Napoleon's invasion of Egypt in 1798. With destiny supposedly on his side, Napoleon mounted his expedition in pursuit of a universal ideal of world conquest. Like Alexander the Great or Caesar Augustus his empire was to bestride both East and West. In was, in Said's words, a 'textual' ambition.

He was steeped in the memories and glories that were attached to Alexander's Orient generally and Egypt in particular. . . . For Napoleon Egypt was a project that acquired reality in his mind and later in the preparations for its conquest, through experiences that belong to the realms of ideas and myths culled from texts, not empirical reality.

And the expedition was to augment the ideas that inspired it. With Napoleon sailed two armies, one of soldiery, the other of scholars and scientists. Physically the Emperor could only conquer, but intellectually he could acquire. The botanists and philologists, historians and antiquarians who were to record and render down the mysteries of the East into manageable academic packages were to take their findings back to France with them. And they did so – to appear in the twenty-three monumental volumes of the

Description de l'Egypte. Though French rule lasted only three years the *Description* represented a generation of scholarship and a unique appropriation of one country by another.

In the nineteenth century Europe's military and technical superiority over the East could at last be taken for granted; the cherished vanity of a millennium had been successfully tested by Napoleon's troops. Affluent, acquisitive and irresistible, the colonial powers henceforth entertained coercion and conquest as legitimate means of policy. But imperialism was not simply or primarily concerned with conquest and empire. It was a system of exploitation and as such gave a higher priority to order than to occupation. To operate successfully European merchants and entrepreneurs required a favourable field with stable conditions, intelligible norms of political behaviour and standard fiscal and property rights. They required immunity from native jurisdiction and protection from local miscreants. And they required financial, commercial and agricultural adjustments to the local economy to adapt it for the world market. Often – and preferably – these conditions could be met without the expense and hostility which conquest entailed. Ideally the methods and manifestations of this hegemony would also tend towards the betterment of the natives and the reduction of strife. But from the laws that were supposed to govern the conduct of prices to the contractual undertakings that were supposed to safeguard commerce, it was Europeans who made the rules. And they were accepted because, in the last analysis, they were enforceable.

Between the French invasion of Egypt in 1798 and the British invasion in 1882 the process of cultural appropriation inaugurated by Napoleon's scholars also made significant progress. This was the age of the Victorian traveller and of the oriental scholar, a few of whom developed a genuine sympathy for the East. J. L. Burchhardt, Edward Lane, Sir Richard Burton, Gifford Palgrave and W. S. Blunt no longer described the Arabs as lecherous bigots. They began to differentiate – city Arabs, desert Arabs, marsh Arabs, *fellahin* – to penetrate Arab society and to appreciate Arab culture. But according to Professor Said this more sympathetic approach was premised on superiority. Enlightened imperialism was still imperialism; without the reality of European hegemony such involvement would have been inadvisable and 'at the crucial instant when an Orientalist had to decide whether his loyalties and sympathies lay with the Orient or with the conquering West, he always chose the latter, from Napoleon's time on'.

Moreover, though the stereotypes might multiply and change, that sense of the East as the reinforcing opposite of European identity remained. Far from being sophisticated the

Arab had now to be portrayed as a political innocent, still at heart one of 'the children of the desert', wayward, naive, impressionable – a fit subject, in other words, for tutelage. The mystery of the East was increasingly reduced to a straight catalogue of vices – dishonesty, cunning, laziness, dirtiness, prostitution. While poets, novelists and artists continued to exploit the more romantic images of the Arabian Nights and the Crusades, imperial proconsuls prided themselves on knowing the reality. To Lord Cromer, who in all but name ruled Egypt for twenty years, the Oriental was a creature to whom, like his camel, certain basic rules of management applied. A lot of work had been done on the subject and Orientals, like camels, had a number of now well established characteristics. The ability to regulate their own affairs was not one of them. In Cromer's book the ludicrous idea of Egyptian nationalism was therefore 'entirely novel' and must be 'of exotic rather than indigenous growth'.

What gave the Oriental's world its intelligibility and identity [writes Edward Said] was not the result of his own efforts but rather the whole complex series of manipulations by which the Orient was identified by the West. Knowledge of the Orient, because generated out of strength, in a sense *creates* the Orient, the Oriental, and his world. In Cromer's and Balfour's language the Oriental is depicted as something one judges (as in a court of law), something one studies and depicts (as in a curriculum), something one disciplines (as in a school or prison), something one illustrates (as in a zoological manual). The point is that in each of these cases the Oriental is *contained* and *represented* by dominating frameworks.

A more pragmatic, less blinkered, appraisal would have revealed that in fact oriental passivity was far from universal. Throughout the nineteenth century the West's supposed 'discovery' of the East was being matched by a cautious but receptive Eastern examination of the West. Increasingly Arab and Turkish scholars and political leaders studied the phenomenon of European power and drew certain conclusions. The first was that Europe's progress owed little to Christianity and was not therefore incompatible with Islam. 'If it [Christianity] were a cause of worldly progress, the Papal states would be the most advanced, not the most backward in Europe,' observed Khayr al-Din, the Tunisian reformer and statesman. The moral superiority of Europe was therefore a fiction.

But in terms of social and technological advance the East had much to learn from the West. After five years in Paris in the 1820s the Egyptian scholar, Rifa'a al-Tahtawi translated Voltaire and Montesquieu and sifted the ideas of the Enlightenment. Without either wholeheartedly embracing European liberalism or rejecting the autocratic pattern of Mameluke and Ottoman rule, he urged that the ruler must be responsive to the wishes and well-being of the people, that political education should be fostered throughout society, and that from it would emerge that sense of common good and national pride which lay at the heart of Europe's achievement.

Other travellers and reformers were more impressed by Europe's technological progress. Ismail Pasha's Minister of Public Works, Ali Mubarak, wrote a novel about his impressions of Europe, published in 1882, in which eighty pages are devoted to the wonders of the steam engine. The telegraph, the railway and the cotton mill were admired and quickly appropriated. Egypt in particular embarked on a programme of rapid modernisation. According to Ali Mubarak, science or knowledge is a universal and cumulative pursuit. It passed from the ancient Egyptians to the Greeks and Romans and then to the Arabs and then to the Europeans. Each in turn had borrowed from its predecessor and as the Arabs had once mastered and extended the discoveries of the Greeks, so now they must master those of Europe.

Within Islamic tradition there was thus a noble precedent for scientific enquiry; and, in the concept of the *umma* (the Muslim community in which all are equal before God) there was an egalitarian principle which seemed to anticipate Western liberal ideology. It was on the basis of reanimating the *umma* that Mohammed Abduh argued at the end of the nineteenth century for the adoption of legal and educational reforms and of some Western principles of government. But the unity of the *umma* was pan-Islamic and international. Nationalist ideology was something different, indeed 'an exotic growth'. However, the aspirations which it clothed were indigenous and, as orientalism became imperialism, increasingly vocal.

It was one thing to admire the technological achievements of the West; it was another to have them mobilised against you. Arab attitudes towards the West reflected – and still reflect – this ambivalence. Palestinian activists like Edward Said hold the West responsible for that most heinous of crimes – the appropriation of the Palestinians' homeland – yet they continue to admire Western institutions and to make the West their haven. The Palestinians in Detroit laud America as the land of the free with as much gusto as did the Jewish refugees from the ghettos of Europe. It goes without saying that their dream of a reclaimed Palestine is of a land in which the liberal freedoms are taken for granted. Even the Palestinian fighters at Beaufort Castle, for all their Third World rhetoric, also dream of a land in which Christian, Muslim and Jew will all live in peace.

A tradition of communal harmony was part of the Palestinian tradition and not the least of the casualties of the last sixty years. It may come as something of a surprise to a Westerner to learn that Edward Said is in fact a Christian; his family were part of Jerusalem's Arab Christian community. And yet he is active for a cause whose principal constituency is Muslim. The point is not simply that nationalism transcends religion but that the fundamental reality for all Arabs and most of all for Palestinians is that Zionism equals Colonialism. In the West Zionism has been consistently represented as a claim on the world's conscience by the Jewish people to a homeland of their own. After the First World War and the Arab Revolt the British, under the Sykes-Picot accord with France, assumed a League of Nations Mandate to regulate the affairs of half the Arab lands conquered from the defunct Ottoman Empire. These lands included Palestine, the ancient Jewish homeland, which – so the argument goes – was now little better than a desert. Magnanimously the British government, in the 1917 declaration by the Foreign Secretary, Arthur James Balfour, had agreed to discharge an international obligation by permitting Jewish refugees to settle there. This gesture was amply rewarded as Jewish settlers poured in during the inter-war years and by dint of great sacrifice and effort made the very desert bloom. After the Second World War and in the face of serious differences between the thrusting Jewish settlers and their resentful Arab neighbours, the British withdrew. The Jewish settlers thereupon accepted a UN partition of Palestine and declared the sovereign state of Israel, successfully repelled an Arab attack on their new-born sovereignty and have continued to do so ever since, acquiring in the process additional territory whose inhabitants were Arabs. Many of these Arabs have preferred to continue the fight in exile and now form the nucleus of a guerrilla organisation called the PLO which has close links with Moscow and with other international guerrilla organisations.

By similar *a priori* reasoning to that used by Lord Cromer to discredit Egyptian nationalism and justify British management of Egypt – i.e. a presumptuous mastery of oriental affairs based on long experience and study – the Palestinian has to be classified as a trouble-maker. He brandishes a gun, screams meaningless slogans and massacres innocent civilians. Like the ruthless Saracen he is, to all civilised and god-fearing men, the epitome of 'otherness'. So too in their different ways – or in juxtaposition to different Western values – are the berobed petro-sheikh and the wretched immigrant worker. And thanks to the press, radio, television and films, these images (and the logic on which they rest) are now more general than ever. But the Israelis are different – or rather more familiar. They have free elections and efficient communications, they invite European orchestras to their capital, watch American TV shows and enter the Eurovision Song Contest. Culturally they belong in the West.

Whether there should be a Western enclave in the heart of the Arab world is not a question that is often asked in the West. Israel is there; it is a political reality and the Arabs had better acknowledge it. But for the Arabs the state of Israel has been something quite different. For them Zionism has not been some unique and unclassifiable world phenomenon but simply an extreme form of colonial appropriation.

It can be expressed most simply in population figures. In 1917 Palestine had a population of about 700,000 of whom about 60,000, or 8%, were Jews, mostly immigrants from Europe over the previous forty years. By 1931 the influx of settlers, again mostly from Europe, had brought the number of Jews up to about 175,000, or about 18%. By 1936 it was 384,000 and by 1946 608,000, or some 30%. In the last years of the British mandate there was some illegal settlement but mostly immigration took place under British auspices and with British and latterly American encouragement. The settlers were not of course British and American citizens, but they had no alternative common national identity and, predominantly Europeans, they were culturally, economically and politically dependants of the West. After the declaration of an Israeli state this dependence intensified. The diplomatic, military and economic support by which the USA underwrites Israel is too well known to need detailing. And the involvement of Israel in a neo-colonial venture like that of the Anglo-French Suez invasion was taken as proof positive that Israel was still a Western puppet, a colonial outpost.

Hence the fighters' talk of 'liberating' Palestine. Hence Yasser Arafat's credentials as the legitimate heir of Ben Bella, Bourguiba and Nasser in the Arab nationalist struggle. And hence the Palestinian conviction that history is on their side.

But there is one big difference between the Palestinian nationalist movement and those of Algeria, Tunisia and Egypt. The Palestinians were not just colonised; most of them were also evicted. Initially probably about 600,000 were forced to leave their homes. With further Israeli colonisation on the West Bank and in the Gaza strip and with a natural increase factor, this figure had risen to about two and a half million refugees by 1975, of whom about one million were still in Israeli held territory.

So much for the statistics. But the tragedy is invariably a personal one. Few people willingly leave their home, their land, their country. 150-200 years ago the Scottish Highlands were cleared to make way for sheep. Just how many Highlanders went is uncertain but the memory of individual evictions, of instances of burning and brutality, still linger, still rankle. In Lebanon, Syria, Jordan, Egypt, the Gulf – in virtually all the Arab countries – in America, Canada, Britain and France – wherever Palestinians have taken refuge – it is the individual tragedies that hurt; the burning of this village, the razing of that, the torture of so-and-so, the massacre at such-and-such, the humiliation of a patriarch, the rape of a sister. Scarcely a family is unscarred and wherever a Palestinian goes, this burden of horror goes with him.

Edward Said asks simply that we acknowledge it, and that we try to understand it as the legacy not of a single generation or a single act of appropriation but as part of a long and continuing East-West confrontation. This might seem to imply a bleak future. But Palestinians cannot afford to be pessimists.

Everyone today, Palestinian and Israeli, Arab and Westerner, lives a life that has been shaped by forces that are larger and deeper in origin than any individual can master. But what such forces as imperialism and nationalism have inscribed in the daily lives of people is a partial recognition that the stranger, the different Other, is a part of a common history which contemporary politics encourage us all to ignore or deny.

Whether to enhance our recognition of the Other or instead to pretend the Other does not exist – that is the question we must consciously face. . . .

Over the years a few courageous voices – scholars, leaders, common people, visionaries, some Arab, some Jewish, some European, some American – have articulated a hope for mutual acknowledgement instead of ignorance and fear, for peace instead of conflict. If, in the long chronicle of war, suffering and partial knowledge, their voices are heard only faintly it is because they belong to a future which we can only faintly perceive at present. But that, I believe, must be the future.

1. *An Israeli soldier before the ruins of Beaufort castle conquered from the Palestinians in June of 1982*

European relations with the Arab world have been dogged and dictated by the need of one civilisation to define itself by reference to another. The Arab or the Oriental has been consistently portrayed as the antithesis of the European. In the Middle Ages this sense of otherness was mainly religious. Islam was seen as a terrifying combination of both heathenism and heresy; the Prophet was 'the Imposter' and his followers – Saracens and Moors – were a threat to all that was Christian and virtuous.

To wrest Jerusalem, a city sacred to Muslims as well as Christians and Jews, from the 'wicked infidels' the first Crusade was despatched in 1096. The three hundred years of sporadic campaigning that followed left their mark on the Middle East in the shape of the Crusader castles which, in the case of Beaufort, are still being fought over today. In Arab eyes the Christian West has never relinquished its claim to regulate the affairs of Palestine, and Israel is but Western interference in a new guise.

2. *From a 13th-century Spanish Chronicle, Arab and Christian knights in battle*

3. *Detail from Horace Vernet's 'The Capture of Abd-el-Kader's Train by the Duc d'Aumale': the 'Attatichs', 1845*

In the nineteenth century, when Europe's military and technical superiority over the East could at last be taken for granted, Europea[n] orientalists moved freely through the Arab world, sometime chronicling European military campaigns (3) but also sometimes portraying a[n] Arab they found sympathetic and intriguing. 'My man took off his coat, jumped on a splendidly harnessed white horse, his arms bare up to th[e] shoulder and laden with gleaming gold weapons, his eyes sparkling, a fresh wound on his handsome face. From that moment I did not leave m[y] hero. If I had been a woman my virtue would have been in serious danger. As it was I made drawings of him from the front, the back, from abov[e] and from below . . .' (From a letter by Vernet describing General Yúsūf)

4. Horace Vernet's 'Jedah and Tamar' (Genesis 38, 13-19), 1840

5. Henri Regnault's 'Summary Execution under the Moorish Kings of Granada', 1860s

6. 'Colonel T. E. Lawrence' by Augustus John

7. Lord Cromer (1841-1917)

Horace Vernet, like Delacroix and Regnault – or like Sir Richard Burton and Charles Doughty – found much to admire in the Arabs. But traits that were the antithesis of those claimed by upright Christian gentlemen were still what was expected of them. The Oriental was portrayed as either inept and naive or cruel and lascivious. In both cases he was a fit subject for a beneficent imperialism.

8. On 6 July 1917 T. E. Lawrence and Auda, a famous tribal leader, made their triumphal entry into Aqaba. The Arabs' seizure of the important port town from the Ottomans ultimately helped advance British and French designs on the region.

'I content myself with noting the fact that somehow or other the Oriental generally acts, speaks and thinks in a manner exactly opposite to the European.' Lord Cromer (7) who for twenty-five years virtually ruled Egypt, perceived the 'otherness' of the East as a wayward contrariness which only firm colonial government could rectify. Lord Balfour (10) took the argument still further and declared that an understanding of the Oriental and of what was in his best interests justified the British presence in Egypt.

This rationale of imperialism, premised by stereotypes of the Oriental as someone fundamentally different and bolstered by the certainty of military, political, economic and even moral superiority, is seen as informing the West's attitude to Arab nationalism during the first half of this century. It is to be found in the pages of (T. E.) Lawrence of Arabia's (6) 'Seven Pillars of Wisdom', in the negotiations with the leaders of the Arab revolt, in the Sykes-Picot agreement by which France and Britain divided Greater Syria after the Revolt, and in Lord Balfour's fateful declaration in favour of Jewish settlement in Palestine.

Foreign Office,
November 2nd, 1917.

Dear Lord Rothschild,

I have much pleasure in conveying to you, on behalf of His Majesty's Government, the following declaration of sympathy with Jewish Zionist aspirations which has been submitted to, and approved by, the Cabinet.

"His Majesty's Government view with favour the establishment in Palestine of a national home for the Jewish people, and will use their best endeavours to facilitate the achievement of this object, it being clearly understood that nothing shall be done which may prejudice the civil and religious rights of existing non-Jewish communities in Palestine, or the rights and political status enjoyed by Jews in any other country".

I should be grateful if you would bring this declaration to the knowledge of the Zionist Federation.

9. The Balfour Declaration, 1917

10. Lord Balfour reviewing the British troops at York Cathedral, 1916

11. Arabs, arrested after riots in Hebron, line up under sub-machine gun. August, 1938

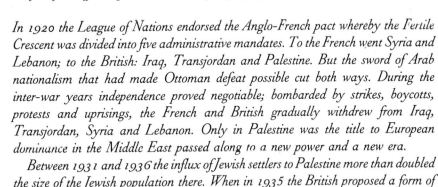

13. A picture found on the body of Nur Ibrahim, a well-known leader of the Arab rebellion. He was killed with four of his staff among the hills north-east of Haifa by a patrol of the West Kents. November, 1938.

In 1920 the League of Nations endorsed the Anglo-French pact whereby the Fertile Crescent was divided into five administrative mandates. To the French went Syria and Lebanon; to the British: Iraq, Transjordan and Palestine. But the sword of Arab nationalism that had made Ottoman defeat possible cut both ways. During the inter-war years independence proved negotiable; bombarded by strikes, boycotts, protests and uprisings, the French and British gradually withdrew from Iraq, Transjordan, Syria and Lebanon. Only in Palestine was the title to European dominance in the Middle East passed along to a new power and a new era.

Between 1931 and 1936 the influx of Jewish settlers to Palestine more than doubled the size of the Jewish population there. When in 1935 the British proposed a form of representative government that would give the Jews eight seats on a legislative council and the Arabs twelve, the Jews rejected it. Though it granted the Jews far greater proportional representation than their numbers justified, it would have fixed an Arab constitutional majority in the independent state that would emerge.

In 1936 the Arabs responded to fears of Jewish expropriation by calling a general strike which in turn became a general Arab rebellion (13). In 1938 the rebellion was renewed with increasing violence when President Roosevelt's conference at Evian failed to find a solution for resettling Jews suffering from Hitler's terror. The United States, Canada and Australia offered to take only a few thousand.

12. Refugees leaving Palestine in 1948 are taken by bus to just inside Jewish fortifications. From there they must go on foot to their new destination in the Arab area.

The virtual occupation of Egypt by Britain lasted seventy-four years and came as inevitably with the opening of the Suez Canal as Pandora's evils. As soon as the Suez Canal became the route to Britain's precious empire in India, neither the French who had engineered it, nor the Egyptians whose sweat had built it and whose land had suffered it, could lay greater claim than the British. When in 1882 Colonel Arabi's 'Egypt for Egyptians' movement prompted the fleet to sail for Port Said, the British responded with a bombardment of Alexandria that lasted ten hours (16).

While Egypt was never formally incorporated into the British Empire, it was, in the words of one of Britain's greatest imperialists, Lord Milner, a Veiled Protectorate. This meant simply that British authority was absolute in most things that mattered until 1936 and that it was still absolute in the region of the Suez Canal until 1956.

Opposition to British rule and to the Kings of Egypt who profited by it (14) intensified after Egypt's brief involvement in the losing battle for Palestine. 'Remember, the real battle is in Egypt,' were the words of one of the war's martyred heroes, Colonel Ahmed Abduk, and Major Gamal Abdul Nasser, who served and was wounded in Palestine, remembered. In 1952, Nasser master-minded a revolution that toppled King Farouk and gave Egyptian rule to native Egyptians for the first time in 2000 years. In 1956 President Nasser oversaw the evacuation of the last British soldier from Egyptian soil at Port Said (17).

14. (right) At the house of the late Saad Zaghoul, founder of the Wafd Party, a schoolgirl stirs a demonstration against the proposed treaty between Great Britain and Egypt.

15. (below left) Scottish troops round the Sphinx after the defeat of Arabi Pasha at the battle of Tel-el-Kebir, 1882

16. (below centre) Alexandria after the bombardment by the British in 1882

17. (below right) Premier Gamal Nasser returns to Cairo after his speech proclaiming the nationalisation of the Suez Canal Company

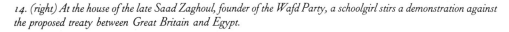

18. A victim of the Algerian war

Excepting Palestine, the French occupation of Algeria must be regarded as the most severe case of colonisation the Arab world was made to suffer. For four generations (1830–1962) the people of Algeria were Gallicized in language and culture and disenfranchised from the government and economy of their country.

Strictly speaking Algeria was not even a French colony – it was a part of France. But the logical consequence of that never followed: until 1947 France consistently refused to grant Algerians full French citizenship unless they renounced their personal status as Muslims. By 1947 it was too late. On May Day in 1945 a peaceful demonstration of Algerian nationalists turned into a riot when police fired on the demonstrators. Colonial troops intervened, bombarding villages and rounding up thousands of people for mass execution (21).

The spread of rebellion and reprisals rendered futile all plans for political reform. Attempts at suppression through the dispatch of a French army a half a million strong and the resettlement of a million and a quarter villagers into guarded enclaves (19) routed much of the revolution's military network. But the rest of the world watched with increasing concern and protestation. Finally Charles de Gaulle, the man least suspected of sympathy for the cause, conceded independence to Algeria.

*...960. In the
...ement camp of El
...French S.A.S.
...rs pose with villagers*

*20. Referendum day in
Algiers. The new nation's
flag flies as Algerians vote
unanimously for
independence and
co-operation with France*

CHAPTER NINE

BUILDING
A NATION

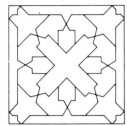 The day they brought us to the beach they brought them all, women, men, old people, children, all. We were surrounded by the sea, the mountains and the skies. They beat them with their bayonets in the stomach. They tied their hands with rope. Here. Then hit them over the head, this way, and told everyone to watch this happening, 'each of you in turn', 'each in turn'. Then at night they came with lorries, took the prisoners, the poor things, out and then brought them here, with spades in hands, and made them dig holes. Then they fired and killed them all, wiped them out – and didn't even bury them, just left them that way.

And then the biggest death toll happened which was worse than the first one. Then there were pregnant women in labour, some women actually gave birth on the sand. There were over ten women who gave birth on the sand – the poor women. And we the prisoners were put in a circle. Somebody called Maurice, the officer in charge, brought in the Foreign Legion and ordered, 'When I say fire, fire. I don't want you to let anyone survive.'

In a series of such incidents during May 1945 the French government made it plain that whatever the future for colonial rule elsewhere in the post-war world, in Algeria there would be no change. France was there to stay. The casualty figures for that fateful month record 103 European deaths and anything between 6,000 and 80,000 Algerian deaths. The precision of the first figure and the wild discrepancies in the second are eloquent testimony to one of the most brutalising and callous conflicts this century has witnessed. Seventeen years later, in 1962, General de Gaulle finally conceded Algerian independence. By then 'about a million' had died as a result of the war. Perhaps a million more had been tortured, maimed, blinded or become deranged, 'about two million' displaced or dispossessed. And all this out of a population of just eight million. Algeria had been mathematically decimated.

Dr Mahfoud Bennoune (born in 1936) comes from a family of eight, two girls and six boys. His village, its tiled roofs banked amidst benign and verdant hills, lies near Constantine to the east of Algeria; it could be Provence.

My father was killed not far from here. My brother also was actually killed in the village; he had already lost his hearing after a battle somewhere which went on for 24 hours. I had another brother who was killed over there in Teshkeef and two more brothers, one of whom was tortured till he became insane; he still lives in the village. The other one also fought as a guerrilla from 1955 through till 1962. He survived. And I also survived. So in this sense I think my father was responsible for all this, in the sense that he really taught us from an early age to think of one thing and to give thought only to one thing – that is to free Algeria.

In terms of social, political and economic dislocation the price of Algerian independence was no less horrifying. Foreseeing the possible difficulties, some Algerian Muslims in the 1930s, though far from being Francophiles, had actually favoured integration with France. On the one hand they conceded the extent of French colonial penetration. Excluding Napoleon's brief adventure in Egypt, it had been Algeria's fate to be the first Arab country to fall under European domination (1830) and the last, excluding Palestine, to throw it off. For four generations this outpost of the Arab-Islamic world was exposed to the full blast of economic exploitation, political emasculation and, above all, the cultural penetration which was the hallmark of the *mission civilisatrice*. On the other hand they also believed Algerian independence would be unsustainable because there was no separate Algerian nation (that is, separate from the universal Muslim *umma*) and there never had been. 'If I had discovered the Algerian nation I would have become a nationalist', declared Ferhat Abbas in 1936. 'I did not discover it. I looked to history. I questioned the living and the dead. I could not find it.'

Strictly speaking Algeria was not even a French colony. With dazzling logic the French decided that a country with no identity of its own would best be served by adopting French identity. Algeria accordingly became a part of France, or rather three *départements* within the French republic. They differed from those of metropolitan France only to the extent that their non-European population enjoyed few of the rights and liberties of French citizenship. But if not a colony, Algeria was colonised – dramatically. Indeed it was the only Arab country, with the exception of Palestine, to be systematically appropriated by European settlement. By the 1950s the number of settlers, or *colons*, was close to a million, a tenth of the total population.

French, of course, was the language of government and the *colons*, of course, enjoyed a monopoly of power. 90% of the top administrative, judicial, industrial and financial jobs were theirs. But they also enjoyed an 80% share of the professions and middle management – bureaucrats, technicians, agriculturalists, teachers and doctors. When during the early 1960s the French settlers packed their bags they made off with the entire human component in the social and economic infrastructure of the country. Algeria was left with hospitals but no doctors, classrooms but no teachers, mines but no engineers, courts but no lawyers.

Paradoxically it was also left with men but no jobs. It needed doctors; it could provide only patients. 90% of the population were illiterate and 80% of the labour force unskilled. A third was unemployed and a further third, mostly seasonal labourers, underemployed. *Colons* had acquired a quarter of the agricultural land – and that much the most productive quarter – thus forcing the peasant farmer on to ever more marginal ground. And, as elsewhere, the birth rate was soaring. Even before the war, refugees from the countryside were swamping the cities of Oran, Algiers and Constantine, giving them some of the highest growth rates – and worst housing – in the world. Emigration offered the only hope and France thus enjoyed a cheap and inexhaustible reservoir of menial manual labour.

Such handicaps were not by any means unique in the Arab world. In the early 1960s Egypt had more pressing demographic problems, the Arabian peninsula was more backward in terms of education and social infrastructure, and the states of the Fertile Crescent could be regarded as more artificially created. The economic viability of Tunisia, Sudan or the Yemens looked more precarious and most Arab states were, and still are, underdeveloped in industrial terms, with the labour force heavily committed to an unprofitable agricultural sector. What distinguished Algeria was a compounding of all these problems together with the prolonged and insidious character of French colonialism and the crisis in Algerian identity. Together they constituted a barrier to independent survival which would surely have proved impenetrable were it not for three important 'plus' factors.

For one thing, French rule could never be accused of having neglected the country. As an important source of raw materials and as a market for manufactured goods, Algeria had been opened up and developed, albeit to French advantage. It had the largest railway network of any Arab or African country, good roads and several airports and harbours. The cities were impressive with fine administrative buildings, cinemas, hospitals, schools and universities. By 1962 there was even a promising, if small and hastily set up, industrial sector. The facilities for development were thus present, if embryonic. The Algerians had to find the skills, the finance, the motivation and the stability to develop them.

Although during the last years of French rule currency fled the country at an alarming rate, development was not to be frustrated by lack of finance. In 1956 the Sahara's resources of oil and, more especially, natural gas were confirmed. Together with important mineral deposits – iron, zinc, bauxite, phosphates – these had, in French eyes, come to represent the main attraction of the country. In French hands they were exploited and, as with the British in Iraq, in French hands they were intended to stay after independence. The possession of much coveted raw materials may be something of a guarantee of economic survival but it is no guarantee of economic or political freedom. The degree to which Algeria was able to exploit its resources beyond outright dependence on foreign skills and investment and the degree to which it was able to resist the blandishments of foreign partners in this development was to be crucial.

Exceptionally handicapped, Algeria in 1962 was also, then, peculiarly favoured. Unlike the other Arab oil exporters – particularly Libya, the Gulf states and Saudi Arabia – it not only had the hydrocarbons but it also had those no less vital resources of manpower, communications and economic structures with which to take advantage of them. More than any other Arab state it had the possibility of performing a sensational leap into the select company of the world's most advanced nations – provided, that is, it could somehow create and sustain its own nationhood. This, at least, was how it looked in 1962.

'We thought that by the 1980s Algeria would have reached the development level of, say, Spain,' recalls Dr Mahfoud Bennoune. In spite of the then unforeseen upsurge in revenues from oil and gas, and in spite of dramatic progress, Algeria is still short of development parity with any European country; but politically it has triumphantly confounded the critics, creating and sustaining a national identity and achieving a degree of stability which must be the envy of many more politically favoured Third World countries. The explanation for both political and economic success lies in the third 'plus' factor in Algeria's inheritance – the revolution itself.

In 1936 Ferhat Abbas had 'questioned both the living and the dead' but still could find no Algerian nation. In 1962 such a poll would have evinced very different results. By then there were cemeteries full of men who if they had lived without a clear national identity, died unequivocally Algerian. And Abbas himself, from championing the cause of assimilation to France, had long since become a convinced nationalist and in fact headed the first Algerian government-in-exile. Resurrected and re-examined, a genealogy of nationalist revolt stretching back to the 1840s and the chivalrous exploits of the Amir Abd al-Qadir were found as precedents. But to a large extent the corporate history of adversity and triumph on which the new nation had to depend had to be concertinaed into the couple of decades that immediately preceded independence.

Unlike Syria, Egypt or Iraq, Algeria could afford no gradual progression from reform to revolt to revolution. It must embrace all three in one gigantic upheaval. By 1963 the Arab path to national credibility was well sign-posted; through Islamic orthodoxy, Arabic culture, social reform and economic planning lay the way ahead. But in Algeria these components, the very bricks of nation-building, were not just lying around waiting to be used. They had to be created. As the medium of education, scholarship, technology and government, French had long since replaced Arabic. As between Berber and Arab – and even as between one Berber tribe and another – it was often the only common language. To forego this pivotal, modern and unifying medium of expression entailed a considerable sacrifice and not only for the educated elite. Moreover, replacing it with Arabic could be seen as an artificial, retrogressive and possibly divisive experiment. Similarly the affirmation of Islamic identity. All Algerians were Muslims but the long tradition of antipathy between the orthodox rationalist *ulama* and the *marabout* orders (local Sufi orders) had been exacerbated by the French blatantly wooing the latter and exploiting their organisation to discredit the former. Suddenly to proclaim the unity and solidarity of the whole Islamic *umma* entailed, in the case of Algeria, another act of faith.

The building bricks of nationhood had thus to be moulded from unstable materials. They endured because, to continue the metaphor, they were baked with a uniquely revolutionary fervour. The roots of the FLN, the National Liberation Front, which led the armed independence struggle, are usually traced back to the Etoile Nord Africaine, a nationalist but also a communist party, founded by emigrant workers in France in 1926. Although the party soon fell out with the French communists, its leadership, in the person of Messali Hadj, remained true to its populist, socialist and radical origins. Messali's radicalism was no less ardent when he adopted pan-Arabism or proclaimed the dignity of Islam and of Arabic culture. With equally powerful rhetoric he also called for the distribution of land to the peasants and inveighed against the evils of imperialism.

During the war itself this revolutionary tendency became much more than rhetoric. Unable to match the military resources of France the Algerians, like the Palestinians today, pursued propagandist policies in which guerrilla tactics on the ground were matched by vigorous diplomacy overseas. The key to success was not to out-fight the French, but to out-organise them. Mobilisation brought with it social reform in the shape of female emancipation and involvement in the struggle. But at the same time anti-Western sentiment inspired a puritanical and fundamentalist interpretation of Islam.

Internationally France's membership of NATO and the fact that NATO weapons were being used against them drew the FLN leadership ever closer to Moscow, Peking and Havana though without diminishing the importance of Nasser's Egypt as the movement's Arabist base and inspiration. 'To me Castro is a brother and Nasser is a teacher,' explained Ahmed Ben Bella, the revolutionary leader who was to emerge as Algeria's first head of state, 'but Tito is an example.' Alignment with revolutionary socialism was expedient in that it internationalised the struggle and won the FLN powerful support. But it was also a genuine reflection of the movement's radical and progressive ideology. Both before and after independence the FLN leadership never tired of emphasising that their battle was for the minds of the people, that the rural peasantry must be mobilised and that revolution was not a once and for all phenomenon but a continuous and sustained process.

As 'the quintessence of a revolutionary polity' (M. C. Hudson) Algeria and its leaders have continued to derive international recognition and domestic legitimacy from the state's impeccable revolutionary credentials. In the 1960s under Ben Bella and his successor, Houari Boumedienne, Algiers became the international free port for separatist, nationalist and leftist dissent. Both men involved themselves in Third World politics and took a leading part in pan-Arab affairs and in the Organisation of African Unity. And Algeria continues to advocate a militant use of the 'oil weapon' and to play a more positive role in the Palestinian struggle than any other non-frontline state.

But political ideology, however egalitarian and appropriate, can hardly win the minds of the people, let alone feed and house them, on its own. The regime and the nation also need tangible achievements in terms of social progress and, above all, economic development. Many emergent nations in the post-colonial period have discovered that the immediate and material aspirations of the people may not be easily reconcilable with the ideological priorities of nationhood. Instant dividends in the form of revenue, consumer goods and even jobs may accrue from throwing the country open to foreign investment, foreign aid and foreign technology. But such assistance invariably brings with it a degree of dependence and manipulation. Succumbing to the temptations of neo-colonialism may create both social and sectorial privilege, abort reform and ultimately provoke reaction. On the other hand an obsession with ideology and an opposition to any foreign involvement may delay development and alienate the people. In either event the prospects for responsive and representative government are diminished and those regimes which lack either a feudal or a charismatic leader drift towards repression and militarism.

Every Arab state has faced this dilemma and none can be said to have entirely resolved it. The fact that even today almost every shade in the spectrum of possible solutions is to be found in operation within the Arab world is proof enough. But it is perhaps encouraging that Algeria, a rank outsider twenty years ago (and still too young for definitive appraisal) is now amongst those who appear closest to success.

A simple explanation of this might be the unexpectedly pragmatic approach of the country's leadership. As one of Ben Bella's aides admitted with astounding frankness: 'in the final analysis we must be strategically revolutionary and tactically neo-colonialist.' Though the FLN could hardly have been more ideologically committed, it came to power with no economic masterplan – a fact that reflected widely divergent views on economic planning within the party – and proceeded to respond to change rather than to direct it. Thus when, on the morrow of independence, agricultural labourers simply took over the management of estates vacated by the *colons*, the government rejoiced at this populist initiative, and encouraged it by making *autogestion*, or worker management, the cornerstone of Algerian socialism. Ownership of such estates rested with the state but it, in return, provided investment, technical and financial advice, marketing arrangements and worker incentives. In spite of this structuring, the principle, so spontaneously asserted, of self-management remained sacrosanct and was soon extended to other state-owned enterprises in industry and commerce. These were, however, few and unintegrated. Just as most land continued to be farmed by its peasant owners so most industry and commerce remained under the control of French and other foreign firms. With the national debt increasing by $20-30 million a month, and with aid and technical assistance pouring in from all over the world but primarily from France, any meddling with French or foreign interests was fraught with dire consequences. In effect 'tactics' were taking priority over 'strategy'. This was the reverse of economic planning and could hardly resolve the appalling social problems of unemployment and lack of skilled personnel. According to Dr Mahfoud Bennoune, the pragmatism of the Ben Bella regime was 'demagogic . . . creeping and short-sighted'. Its failure contributed directly to the military coup of 1965 which brought Boumedienne to power.

At first the new regime was too concerned with establishing its authority within the FLN and the country to undertake any drastic restructuring. But in the late 1960s and throughout the 1970s Belaid Abdeslam, the radical Minister of Industry and Energy, launched the country on a series of planned development programmes designed to industrialise the economy and set a new precedent for Third World development. Having compressed the process of reform, revolt and revolution into a couple of decades, Algeria was now about to squeeze the Industrial Revolution into a similar time slot.

The question was how to start the development of a country. Do you start with the end process which is the establishment of a light consumer goods industry? Or do you start from the beginning of the industrial process which is basic industries like steel, engineering and cement? And if you start with the end process and import the machines and materials to sustain it, will you ever be able to work back to the base? This has been the debate throughout the Third World, especially in Latin America.

In Algeria there was no alternative to industrialisation and, given the resources available and given the size of the problems facing the country, the only realistic option was to start from the beginning which is the establishment of basic industries. In time this would generate and stimulate the growth of light industries and agricultural production. It would take a great deal of capital investment; steel furnaces cost more than the machinery needed for light industry. But within twenty years from the beginning of the process we would be producing our own capital equipment and within a second generation, that is within forty years, we will have reached the stage of industrial development where the country is capable of producing its own means of production. This will stimulate a variety of ancillary services and industries and it is in these that employment will be created.

Dr Bennoune characterises this approach as 'based upon a model of unbalanced sectorial growth,' the model being that of Russia where an industrial base had been created out of nothing during the 1920s, 'one of the most successful rapid industrialisations in the modern world,' and the imbalance being in favour of basic industries – steel, engineering, construction materials, chemicals and petrochemicals – over agriculture, light industries and services. It goes without saying that the state's role was to be all-pervasive. The four-year plans meant not just state planning of the economy but state management as evidenced by the rapid nationalisation of all foreign concerns and of all financial houses, ownership of all major industries, the setting up of state-run conglomerates like Sonatrach which controls the extraction and conversion of all hydrocarbons, and the monopoly of all import and export activities. It looked like the triumph of Marxist ideology and an outright rejection of 'tactical neo-colonialism'.

But it was also a logical and pragmatic solution in Algeria's peculiar circumstances. The resources of oil and gas which were to be used to finance development were finite. If the country was ever to achieve an industrial base it had to move quickly. To guarantee prompt implementation both the workers' management committees of *autogestion* and the foreign owned subsidiaries of neo-colonialism had to be taken over; it was a matter of expediency as much as ideology. But this did not mean an end to foreign involvement. Technical assistance, investment aid and capital equipment were solicited from both East and West. Though France declined as Algeria's major trading partner, this position was taken over by the United States.

Although Dr Bennoune believes that industrialisation was the only option, the regime was never unanimously committed to it. Within the government the ministries of Finance and Planning opposed the whole idea of unbalanced sectorial growth; and no doubt their attempts to discredit it would have succeeded in Boumedienne's lifetime had the policy not been an undeniable success. In effect industrialisation, through the allocation of ever more development funds to petrochemicals, steel etc., was pursued because it seemed to work. The regime desperately needed the legitimacy that accrues from performance. Likewise the nation as a whole needed the reassurance of positive achievement. By emphasising that true independence would only be achieved through the economic self-sufficiency that comes with a broad industrial base, the regime was able to still expectations of instant betterment, redirect the blast of revolutionary fervour and dedicate an entire decade (1969-79) to industrialisation.

The success of this policy can be judged in many ways. There are the refineries, steel works, chemical plants and heavy engineering complexes which make Algeria one of the most industrially advanced countries in the Third World. There are the statistics – an average annual growth rate in the industrial sector of around 10%, in the gross domestic product of 6.2% (1970-76) and in the non-agricultural labour force of 11%. And there is the reality of the Algerian home with its television, its cooker, its refrigerator all made in Algeria by Algerians from Algerian-made components. In the fields Algerian tractors spread Algerian fertilisers and in the cities Algerian steel reinforces Algerian concrete.

By the standards of more advanced nations, the factories may be abysmally managed, overmanned, underproductive, cursed with an appalling accident rate and environmentally disastrous. The tractors may be as unreliable as the statistics and as scarce as the fertiliser. But organisation, design and efficiency can be regarded as refinements. As in the business of nation-building, Algeria has had to bake the bricks of industrialisation as well as assemble them. To forge steel the peasant worker has to acquire certain skills and to acquire these he must at least be literate. He also has to acquire new working habits entailing such things as punctuality, factory discipline and operational co-ordination. The switch from an agricultural economy to an industrial one has enormous social ramifications which may well prove to be the real bonus of such precipitate development.

For instance the pace of expansion in both higher and basic education has certainly been forced by industrialisation. With unemployment in the agricultural sector three times higher than that in the industrial sector the message was clear. 80% of school age children now attend school and with Arabic the medium of instruction 80% of this new generation are subscribing to Arabic as the common national heritage. It is often argued that Algeria's obsession with economic development has made it the most culturally emasculated and uninteresting of all the Arab states. This would be worth examining if indigenous culture had been thriving before independence. In fact there was no such thing; the real culprit was not industrialisation but colonisation. Algeria is having to recreate its cultural identity as part of its national identity. Any process which encourages education and finances the dissemination of Arab-Islamic values is a cultural boon. Some of the newspapers are still published in French and French is still the first language of the educated elite of the pre-independence generation. But a transformation is well under way. The fact that television programmes are in Arabic may be more significant than that the set itself is made in Algeria.

By definition any advocacy of unbalanced sectorial growth implies the temporary neglect of other sectors. Industrialisation has certainly had its casualties, most notably in the failure to satisfy housing needs, improve communications and, above all, develop agriculture. Agricultural production has actually declined since independence and, with one of the highest birth rates in the world, Algeria now has to import even basic foodstuffs. Recognising the problem, the Algerian government, under the five-year plan adopted in 1980, has opted for 'accommodation', with industrial output being directly geared to social needs and development priority being given to housing, farming and the social infrastructure.

To some this is further evidence of welcome flexibility and pragmatism but to Dr Bennoune it is a premature reversal, and so a disastrous betrayal, of industrialisation. 'The full maturation of an industrial development requires at least forty years. To nip the process in the bud constitutes a monumental error because it not only destroys the chances of development but demoralises the whole nation.'

No country can less afford demoralisation than Algeria. But Dr Bennoune's plea is relevant not just for his own country but for all the Arab states and for the whole developing world. The 70% of the world's population who live in the Third World countries consume just 6% of the world's main industrial resources (compared with 26% by the socialist bloc and 68% by the West). So long as this sort of imbalance continues, he argues, poverty, exploitation and unrest will be the lot of the Third World. Without developing its own industrial base no Third World country will ever for long be master of its own destiny. Algeria is poised to break out of this mould. But further progress seems dependent on a rekindling of ideological fervour and a change in the practice of government.

I believe (writes Dr Bennoune) that social justice will prevail only in an industrial economy, which can't be attained without democracy. Democracy, in its broad sense, is not only a moral imperative but a necessary condition for a rational management of a developing society. Democracy makes those in power accountable. This would not only reduce injustice and errors of judgement, but also corruption and nepotism. Democracy promotes competence, efficiency and a division of labour based on merit, professionalism and technical skill. Development and democracy go together. Underdevelopment breeds only tyranny and stagnation.

1. August 1982, Beirut under Israeli bombardment.

For many Arabs, Beirut is the stage on which the crisis of their political identity has been played out in its starkest (most Kafka-esque) form. Historical ironies are so thickly layered in the city streets that they can be read like geological strata. In Martyr's Square, central Beirut (2), a statue in memory of Arab nationalists who were hanged by the Turkish Ottomans in 1916 and 1917 is surrounded by the skeletal remains of buildings blasted in the civil war of 1975-77. The whole forms a gruesome backdrop for a Lebanese family photograph.

The Lebanese civil war, itself an endless series of Chinese boxes – Western capitalism vs. socialism; Christian isolationism vs. pan-Arabism; Christian vs. Muslim; Israel vs. Syria – was nevertheless seen by many Arabs to be the grotesque articulation of a political debate which has, at one time or another, engaged every Arab. And the 1982 Israeli bombardment of Lebanon (1) has also symbolized the real impotence of Arab governments.

2. (on facing page) Martyr's Square, Beirut, Lebanon; 3. (below) Lebanese children wearing 'Star Wars' masks play in the ruins of the civil war

4. *A weekly recording of Arab music at the television studio in Jeddah, Saudi Arabia*

The Arabs are politically and socially disparate; if there is still a common bond it is largely due to a cultural fluidity which applies equally to publishing, the media, the arts and to scholarship. Such cultural interchange has always been a feature of the Arab-Islamic world. But its scale and penetration in the Arab world of today is wholly unprecedented. Because of mass media and the spread of literacy, the voice of the writer, the singer, the actor, crosses all the boundaries of Arab nation-states and political allegiances.

5. Cairo, 1975. Hundreds mourn the death of Umm Khalthoum, a singer whose songs were written by Egypt's finest contemporary poets and musicians

6. *Gamal Ahmed al-Ghitani, a prominent Egyptian novelist and short-story writer and one of several Arab writers who are called 'The Generation of the Sixties', with Basim Musallam*

'When one now meets a friend from Morocco or a friend from Syria, or a friend from Beirut, one has a whole cultural heritage and a long background in common. Add to this the fact that in the modern present time a writer, for example, who cannot publish in his own country can have his work published in another. (This is so) because 150 million people write and speak Arabic. So if he cannot publish in his own country, for any reason, he can have his work published in Beirut. I speak from personal experience ... Najib Mahfuz, the well-known Egyptian novelist, did not become known in the Arab Maghreb except through Beirut.'

7. *Duraid Laham, a popular Syrian actor, director and writer of comic satire*

'When a 'Toast to the Homeland' was shown in Tunisia, people thought that the play was written for Tunisia as if I had been living there. But in fact I never went to Tunisia before the opening of the play. This, of course, shows how similar are our lives in the Arab states in particular and the Third World in general as far as the problem of the relationship between regimes and citizens is concerned. . . . Perhaps the problem is not with the regimes, it is rather with the executive authorities which always make mistakes. . . The problem, for example, concerns freedom of expression. This freedom could be 50% here and 40% in another country but it is an existing problem in varying degrees.'

8. *Beirut, Lebanon: The Arab Press*

One of the common denominators of Arab cultural expression is the theme of political repression. Ironically, the practice of censorship in some countries has forced the native writer to forge even stronger links with the Arab world beyond his boundaries

CONCLUSION:
THE ARABS
NOW

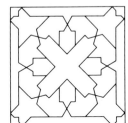Politically the Arab World today is a landscape of division – of opposing groups and interests. We observe the manifest inability of the Arab States to adopt common or effective policies on the core Arab issues, like Palestine; and the habit of various regimes each to follow its own narrowly defined state interest. There is nothing new in this, and dwelling on the current political differences among the Arabs will generate very little understanding of new developments in the Arab world. There are those who talk about the Arab world as if it has existed, from time immemorial, as a whole, united structure, and use the evidence of Arab difference and confusion to support the false but common notion that it is now collapsing or disintegrating. On the contrary, an Arab world in which people in Morocco, for example, can easily understand the colloquial dialect of Egyptians, and in which 30 million school children learn the same language and acquire the same set of historical and cultural references, is a new achievement of the twentieth century. The Arabs, through cultural and economic activity, have been forging new connections that simply did not exist even in the great age of Arab empire. The modern Arab world is a structure that is being built (though it is still far from completion), and whose potential for integration and unity is only now beginning to emerge.

It is impossible to understand the present mood of political frustration, defeatism and impotence among Arabs without reference to the climate of optimism, political movement, even adventurism that existed only twenty years ago. The 1950s and 60s were the period during which the peoples of the Third World asserted themselves against the exhausted empires of England and France, and claimed a rightful place in the community of nations. From India to Egypt, and from Vietnam to Algeria, native societies rose to assert their right to self-determination, to economic development and social justice. These political objectives motivated the Arab peoples and channelled their hopes and struggle. The ideas of Arab nationalism and unity, which until then had been the province of some intellectuals and small political parties (mostly in Lebanon, Syria, Jordan and Iraq), suddenly gained great political importance when Egypt, the central Arab State, adopted them as government policy. The conversion of the revolutionary

9. A classroom in Morocco. In the whole Arab region school enrolment increased by 57% in the first seven years of the 1970s and the new literacy is Arab literacy

Egyptian regime under Nasser to Pan-Arabism, and its active projection of Arab unity as state policy, gave the Arabs and the world the impression that unity was a practical, realisable objective. The Union between Egypt and Syria into the United Arab Republic of 1958-61 seemed like the first step in an inexorable process.

While in the last decade similar schemes for Arab unity have no longer been taken seriously, twenty years ago unity was viewed with either millenial hope or genuine fear. And yet Nasser's policy rested on relatively weak foundations, and both the hopes and fears were exaggerated. After his departure the Arabs have gone on to try completely different policies from his, and as these new policies have failed to achieve positive results, Nasser's basic political position has remained an attractive alternative. This political position involved the following principles: that the Arabs ought not to be aligned with either superpower; that they should have control over their own wealth and resources; and that they should seek to achieve social and economic justice for every citizen of the Arab world.

Few would challenge the description of Nasser as a patriot and a nationalist who stood against foreign interference in Egypt and the Arab world, but Nasser was not a democrat. Patriotic and well-meaning Egyptians and other Arabs had reason to oppose him on that point alone. Still others were convinced that the Egyptian espousal of Pan-Arabism was nothing more than a policy to further Egypt's own interest in the Arab world. There were enough elements of truth in this last opinion to lead to the break-up of the United Arab Republic in 1961. This followed from Syrian revolt against what they perceived to be high-handed Egyptian dominance.

Nasser's Arab project was finally destroyed when Israel attacked and defeated the armies of Egypt, Syria and Jordan in 1967. The combined forces of Israel, the West and anti-Nasser Arabs put Nasser and the Egyptian regime back 'in their place', and introduced into Egyptian politics the fateful seeds of pragmatism and defeatism. President Sadat, who ruled Egypt after Nasser's death in 1970, nurtured the growth of these seeds into fully-fledged policies; under his leadership Egypt abandoned the Arab cause and consigned itself to dependence on the United States.

Nothing shows how fragile the foundations of Nasser's Arab policies were more than the ease with which Sadat was able to reverse them. It is a great paradox that today the Arab world is much more solidly integrated economically, socially and culturally than it ever was in Nasser's time. Indeed this integration happened with great speed in the decade that followed his departure from the scene. Compared to conditions today the connections between the various Arab societies were relatively underdeveloped twenty years ago, and it is possible to argue that political Arabism had peaked too soon. Arabism as defined then was an underdeveloped and immature political idea.

The population of the Arab world increased by thirty-three percent between 1970 and 1979, from 120 million to about 160 million. Not only are there more Arabs now than there were a few decades ago, but there are more Arabs aware of their Arabness. Fifty years ago one could not really say that there was a unity of consciousness among Arabs from Baghdad to Casablanca, from Beirut and Damascus to Cairo, Kuwait to Algeria. But education and modern communications have moved Arabs to share each other's history and experience. All Arabs are watching the same series on television. In schools the same classical material is at the core of the curriculum of many different Arab educational systems. On a more advanced level the same core curriculum occupies the attention of professors and students at the burgeoning Arab universities. In the creative literary arts – poetry, the novel, short story and journalistic article – there is one contemporary Arabic literature. This unifying cultural activity has been going on for a hundred years. But it has speeded up considerably in the last two decades. In only seven years (1970-77) the number of Arabs in school increased fifty-seven percent from 16.3 million to 25.6 million, and the number of teachers by an even greater percentage (79 percent) to a figure of 1,014,000. Today there are over thirty million Arabs in school, and another thirty million who are high school or university graduates. The existence of such a large educated citizenry is a new phenomenon. It would be surprising indeed if the demands for political participation by this new educated class did not produce changes in the Arab ruling establishments which have not yet accommodated themselves to the new conditions.

There is new and growing Arab interdependence. The best example is the massive labour migrations from countries such as Egypt, Yemen, Jordan/Palestine, Syria, Lebanon and Tunisia to the oil-rich Arab countries. In many ways the Egyptian case is the most telling. In 1968 only 10,000 Egyptians were granted permits to work abroad, but the number of permits increased fiftyfold – to 500,000 in 1978. In 1983 it was estimated that over three million Egyptians were working in other Arab countries. Cairo airport at any one day is filled with 3,000 Egyptians leaving to go to Iraq or Saudi Arabia or Libya, and hundreds returning. The remittances of Egyptian workers to their families at home, and the monies they bring back upon their return, have created new patterns of consumption which are daily transforming Egyptian society. The Open Door economic policy of the Sadat regime could not have been sustained without the conditions made possible by this migration (remittances in hard currency rose from $10 million in 1970 to

$2,000 million in 1979 – a two hundred fold increase!), and by the more general economic transformation of the Arab world which the influx of oil money in the 70s made possible.

This Arab labour migration has some special characteristics which are worth noting. The migrants represent a complete cross section of the Egyptian labour force, from ex-generals and ministers who act as advisors on the highest levels of the rich host countries, university professors and high school teachers, journalists who help run the mass media – newspapers, radio and television; to skilled labour such as construction workers, electricians and mechanics, right through to unskilled labour at the other end of the spectrum. This is quite unlike the Turkish labour migration to Germany, or the Algerian to France, or the Mexican to the United States. For the Arab labour migrants into other Arab countries move to societies which use the same language, and they help run everything, including all departments of government. With the exception of the ruling establishment, they can enter every sphere of the new society's life.

The economies of labour-exporting and host Arab countries have become dependent on the inter-Arab labour migration to such an extent that labour movement (as well as the movement of Arab capital) seems to have become independent of Arab politics-as-usual. When war broke out between Egypt and Libya in July 1977, neither Qaddafi nor Sadat dared tamper with the labour links between Egypt and Libya. The 400,000 Egyptians working in Libya were not asked to leave by either party. And again after Sadat's peace treaty with Israel, hostile Arab reaction and reprisals against Egypt did not include boycott of Egyptian labour, possibly the only effective sanction against Sadat. As Saad Eddin Ibrahim, author of *The New Arab Social Order* observed, 'Gone are the days when one Arab ruler could send home the citizens of another wholesale, or [when one could] withdraw his citizens wholesale in retaliation.'

The flow of labour is easier to measure than the flow of ideas, styles of life, or the broadening and sharing of concerns. One could go today to the smallest village in Egypt and ask the postman what kind of mail he handles, and he would report that people receive letters from Saudi Arabia, from Bahrain, or Morocco. It is not too much to imagine these names were never uttered in Egyptian peasant circles fifteen years ago. Nasser had much less to work with when he launched his policies a quarter of a century ago.

* * *

Cultural and economic integration notwithstanding, there is daily evidence of the lack of political co-operation. As we have seen, to most Arabs, there is no issue which brings their political failures into greater focus than the problem of Palestine. Israel has been able to achieve important successes as a result of its strength and conquests. It has signed a peace treaty with Egypt and, after the 1982 invasion, a favourable agreement with Lebanon. These agreements have been concluded in neglect of the essential Palestinian-Israeli problem which only a separate Palestinian state on the West Bank can resolve. For with the Israeli victory in 1967, Palestine was returned to a situation similar to that which existed in the 1940s, before the establishment of Israel: two populations, one Arab and one Jewish, were circumscribed within the same territory, both claiming it as their exclusive homeland. The difference is that the ratio of the two populations has changed. In the 1940s the Palestinians outnumbered Jews three to one; now Israelis outnumber Palestinians three to two. In the final analysis the Israelis have one of two choices. They can try to dominate their Palestinian population indefinitely, or they can reach agreement with them. The price of that agreement will be Palestinian statehood.

The importance of Palestine in the context of this discussion lies not simply in what it reveals of Arab political failures, but in what light it sheds on the current ideology of Arab statehood. Independent statehood is the *sine qua non* of twentieth-century history and it is this that has led most Palestinians to accept the existence of Israel in return for the creation of a Palestinian mini-state in the West Bank, beside Israel. If nothing else, this would gain them a passport and legal identity like their neighbours. Modern Arab political thought, when it concentrated on political unity, tended to overlook the importance of the separate Arab states. These states have provided the essential framework for all the developments of the twentieth century, and, given the exigencies of modern history, the fact that Palestinians have not been able to gain their statehood must be seen as a political failure internationally shared.

As we have seen in Algeria and Kuwait, but also elsewhere in the Arab world, the oil money of the last few decades has helped to finance an impressive new edifice of material progress. The Arab world as a whole has tripled its income in the last ten years and has invested heavily in the construction of roads and airports, electrification of the countryside, distribution of water, building of schools, training of manpower, and the construction of industrial plants. The development of an economic superstructure is only a part, but it is an important part, of the creative activity which has increasingly engaged the citizens of Arab states. For the generations of Palestinians born without this, the loss is acutely imagined; for the Lebanese more recently deprived of this, the loss is all too measurably in view. And so, even in Beirut, in many ways the birthplace of modern Arabism, the majority of Lebanese have been persuaded by recent experience that their most immediate task should be to reconstruct the independent Lebanese state. It is becoming increasingly apparent that the really important issue is whether the separate Arab states can meet the needs and aspirations of their citizens.

BIBLIOGRAPHY

Abu-Lughod, J.L., *Cairo, 1001 Years of the City Victorious* (Princeton, 1971)

—, 'Migrant Adjustment to City Life: The Egyptian Case', *Peasant Society, a Reader*, eds J.M. Potter, M.N. Diaz and George M. Foster (Boston, 1967)

Adams, C.C., *Islam and Modernism in Egypt* (London, 1933)

Amin, Galal, *The Modernisation of Poverty* (Leiden, 1980)

Arberry, A.J., *Aspects of Islamic Civilisation as Depicted in the Original Texts* (London, 1964)

Barbour, N., *Morocco* (London, 1965)

Beck, L. and Keddie, N.R. (eds), *Women in the Muslim World* (Boston, 1978)

Berques, J., *Cultural Expression in Arab Society Today* (Texas, 1978)

—, *Egypt: Imperialism and Revolution* (London, 1972)

Buheiry, M.(ed.), *Intellectual Life in the Arab East, 1890-1939* (Beirut, 1981)

Cheyne, A.G., *The Arabic Language; Its Role in History* (Minnesota, 1969)

Coon, C.S., *Caravan: The Story of the Middle East* (London, 1952)

Daniel, N., *The Cultural Barrier* (Edinburgh, 1975)

Dodd, E.C. and Khairwallah, *The Image of the Word* (Beirut, 1981)

Gabrielli, F., *The Arab Revival* (London, 1961)

Gibb, H.A.R., *Modern Trends in Islam* (Chicago, 1945)

—, *Mohammedanism; an Historical Survey* (Oxford, 1969)

Gilsenan, M., *Saint and Sufi in Modern Egypt* (Oxford, 1973)

—, *Recognising Islam: An Anthropologist's Introduction* (London, 1982)

Gordon, D.C., *The Passing of French Algeria* (London, 1966)

Grabar, O., *The Formation of Islamic Art* (Yale, 1973)

Graziani, J.S., *Arabic Medicine in the Eleventh Century as Represented in the Works of Iqn Jaẓalah* (Karachi, 1980)

Hayes, J.R., (ed.) *The Genius of Arab Civilisation* (New York, 1975)

Hitti, P.K., *Capital Cities of Arab Islam* (Minneapolis, 1973)

—, *Makers of Arab History* (London, 1969)

Holt, P.M., Lewis, B., and Lambton, A., (eds), *The Cambridge History of Islam*, 3 vols (Cambridge, 1970)

Hourani, A., *Arabic Thought in the Liberal Age* (London, 1962)

—, and Stern, S.M. (eds), *The Islamic City* (Oxford, 1970)

Hudson, M.C., *Arab Politics; The Search for Legitimacy* (New Haven, 1977) al-Husry, K.S., *Origins of Modern Arab Political Thought* (New York, 1980)

Ibn Battuta, *Travels*, ed. H.A.R. Gibb (Cambridge, 1958)

Ibn Khaldun, *The Muqaddimah*, ed. N.J. Dawood (London, 1967)

Ibrahim, S.E., *The New Arab Social Order* (London, 1982)

Julian, P., *The Orientalists, European Painters of Eastern Scenes* (Oxford, 1977)

Keddie, N.R. (ed.), *Scholars, Saints and Sufis* (Berkeley, 1972)

Khatibi, A.K. and Sijelmussi, M., *The Splendours of Islamic Calligraphy* (London, 1976)

Lapidus, I.M. (ed.), *Middle Eastern Cities* (Los Angeles, 1964)

Laroui, A., *The Crisis of the Arab Intellectual* (Los Angeles, 1976)

Le Tourneau, R., *Fez in the Age of the Marinides* (Oklahoma, 1961)

Lewis, B. (ed.), *The World of Islam; Faith, People, Culture* (London, 1976)

Makdisi, G., *The Rise of the Colleges; Institutions of Learning in Islam and the West* (Edinburgh, 1981)

Mansfield, P., *The Arabs* (London, 1976)

Musallam, B.F., 'Birth Control in Middle Eastern History', in *The Islamic Middle East, 700-1900; Studies in Economic and Social History*, ed. A.L. Udovitch (Princeton, 1980)

—, 'Power and Knowledge', *Merip Reports*, no.79 (June, 1979)

—, *Sex and Society in Islam; Birth Control Before the Nineteenth Century* (Cambridge, 1983)

Nasir, S.J., *The Arabs and the English* (London, 1979)

Nasr, H., *Islamic Science* (London, 1976)

O'Brien, P., *The Revolution in Egypt's Economic System* (London, 1966)

Ostle, R.C. (ed.), *Studies in Modern Arabic Literature* (London, 1975)

Owen, R., *The Middle East in the World Economy, 1800-1914* (London, 1981)

Radwan, S., *Capital Formation in Egyptian Industry and Agriculture, 1882-1967* (London, 1974)

Rodinson, M., *The Arabs* (London, 1981)

Rogers, M., *The Spread of Islam* (Oxford, 1976)

Rugh, W.A., *The Arab Press* (London, 1979)

Said, E., *Orientalism* (London, 1978)

—, *The Question of Palestine* (London, 1980)

Saliba, G., 'The Development of Astronomy in Medieval Islamic Society', *ASQ*, vol.4, no.3 (1982)

Sayigh, Y.A., *The Arab Economy, Past Performance and Future Prospects* (Oxford, 1982)

Sergeant, R.B. (ed.), *The Islamic City* (Paris, 1980)

Ullmann, M., *Islamic Medicine* (Edinburgh, 1978)

Vatikiotis, P.J., *The Modern History of Egypt* (London, 1969)

Waddy, C., *Women in Muslim History* (London, 1980)

Waterbury, J., *Hydro-Politics of the Nile Valley* (New York, 1979)

Zeine, N.Z., *Arab-Turkish Relations and the Emergence of Arab Nationalism* (Beirut, 1958)

INDEX

ACKNOWLEDGEMENTS

CHAPTER 1 1,H.Winter/Zefa; 2,Sounak/Zefa; 3,K.Goebel/Zefa; 4,Croxford/Zefa; 5,John Topham Picture Library; 6,Nic Wheeler/Mepha; 7,R.Bond/Zefa; 8,Gianni Tortoli/Colorific; 9,Anthony Howarth/Susan Griggs Agency; 10,Liba Taylor/Xenon; 11,F.Jackson/Robert Harding Associates; 12,Geoff Dunlop; 13,Jon Gardey/Robert Harding Associates; 14,Gianfranco Gorgoni/Contact/Colorific; 15,Jon Gardey/Robert Harding Associates; 16,J.Bitsch/Zefa.

CHAPTER 2 1,F.Jackson/Robert Harding Associates; 2,3,4,all Roger Banning/Kufic Films; 5,6,Bibliotheque Nationale, Paris (Ms 5847, fol 69v & 5v); 7,Victor Englebert/Susan Griggs Agency; 8,Geoff Dunlop.

CHAPTER 3 1,Abdal Ghaffur Mould/NAAS; 2,3,R.J.Searight Collection, London; 4,Chris Parker/Alan Hutchison Library; 5,6,7,8,all Roger Banning/Kufic Films; 9,10,11,all Geoff Dunlop; 12,Michael Yorke; 13,Geoff Dunlop; 14,Ian Yeomans/Daily Telegraph Colour Library.

CHAPTER 4 1,Georg Gerster/John Hillelson Agency; 2,3,4,all Roger Banning/Kufic Films; 5,David Collison; 6,Roger Banning/Kufic Films; 7,8,Roland and Sabrina Michaud/John Hillelson Agency; 9,Bruno Barbey/Magnum; 10,Guy le Querrec/Magnum; 11,12,13,14,15,16,17,18,19,all Roger Banning/Kufic Films.

CHAPTER 5 1,Ian Yeomans/Susan Griggs Agency; 2,John Whitfield/The Photographers' Library; 3,Geoff Dunlop; 4,K.Scholz/Zefa; 5,Liba Taylor/Xenon; 6,Mike Fox; 7,Y.G.Berges/Sygma/John Hillelson Agency; 8,Maiofiss/Gamma; 9,Tor Eigeland/Susan Griggs Agency; 10,John Dollar.

CHAPTER 6 1,British Library (Ms Or 2784, fol 96); 2,M.Hackforth-Jones/Robert Harding Associates; 3,David Holden/Robert Harding Associates; 4,Roger Banning/Kufic Films; 5, Bodleian Library, Oxford (Ms Fraser 201, fol 1014r); 6,Bodleian Library, Oxford (Ms Hunt 156, fol 85v); 7,Roger Banning/Kufic Films; 8,Geoff Dunlop; 9,10,11,all Roger Banning/Kufic Films; 12,Bodleian Library, Oxford (Ms Pococke 375, fol 3v-4r); 13,Bodleian Library, Oxford (Ms Or 3222, fol 105r).

CHAPTER 7 1,John Dollar; 2,Abdal Ghaffur Mould/NAAS; 3,Mike Fox; 4,J.Frosting/Mepha; 5,Christine Osborne; 6,Kay Muldoon/Colorific; 7,Adam Woolfitt/Susan Griggs Agency; 8,Kay Muldoon/Colorific; 9,John G.Ross/Susan Griggs Agency; 10,Liba Taylor/Xenon; 11,B.Lyons/Mepha; 12,Barry Ackroyd.

CHAPTERS 8/9 1,Geoff Dunlop; 2,Biblioteca de Escorial; 3,Chateau de Versailles/Giraudon, Paris; 4,Wallace Collection, London; 5,The Louvre/Giraudon, Paris; 6,John Webb/Tate Gallery, London; 7,Evelyn Baring/BBC Hulton Picture Library; 8,Imperial War Museum, London; 9,British Library; 10,Keystone Press; 11,Library of Congress, Washington DC/Angela Murphy; 12,P.Guldman/ Popperfoto; 13,Popperfoto; 14,15,16,all BBC Hulton Picture Library; 17,Keystone Press; 18,Marc Flament/Rapho, Paris; 19,Nicholas Tikhomiroff/Magnum; 20,Popperfoto; 21,22,both Etablissement Cinematographique et Photographique des Armées, Paris.

CHAPTER 10 1,Neveu Liaison/Gamma; 2,3,Fouad Khoury/Sygma; 4,Peter Carmichael/Aspect Picture Library; 5,Robin Constable/Alan Hutchison Library; 6,David Collison; 7,Mike Fox; 8,Christine Osborne; 9,Bruno Barbey/Magnum.

The publishers would also like to thank Ann Bridges and Val Hansen for their help in this project. Picture research by Angela Murphy.